D0970546

NOV 2 1 2013

A GANNETT COMPANY

Lifeline
BIOGRAPHIES

KANYE WEST
Soul-Fired Hip-Hop

by Kayla Morgan

Twenty-First Century Books · Minneapolis

Twenty-First Century Books
A division of Lerner Publishing Group, Inc.
241 First Avenue North
Minneapolis, MN 55401 U.S.A.

Website address: www.lernerbooks.com

Library of Congress Cataloging-in-Publication Data

Morgan, Kayla.
    Kanye West : soul-fired hip-hop / by Kayla Morgan.
        p.   cm. — (USA Today lifeline biographies)
    Includes bibliographical references and index.
    ISBN 978-0-7613-8640-7 (lib. bdg. : alk. paper)
    1. West, Kanye. 2. Rap musicians—United States—Biography—Juvenile literature.
I. Title.
ML3930.W42M67 2013
782.421649092—dc23 [B]   2011052447

Manufactured in the United States of America
1 – PP – 7/15/12

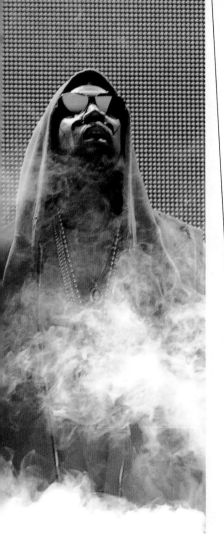

INTRODUCTION

Kings: Kanye West *(left)* performs with hip-hop legend Jay-Z in 2011 during their Watch the Throne Tour.

In the Spotlight

■■■■

When the lights go down in the massive auditorium and the spotlights flow onto the stage, Kanye West feels right at home. Waiting backstage to make his entrance, he begins to move to the sound of his own special hip-hop beats, listening to the cheering fans that await him. The young crowd filling Philips Arena in Atlanta, Georgia, grows more and more energized, eager for the moment when the rapper will appear.

Tonight, Kanye will not take the stage alone. His friend and fellow hip-hop artist Jay-Z stands alongside him. It is October 28, 2011, the debut concert for their Watch the Throne Tour.

The scene is set for a huge, dynamic show. Two smaller, cube-shaped stages sit next to the main stage. Soon Kanye will stand on these pedestals and sing. Large video screens project a giant image of his face as he leaps out from backstage, arms raised. A laser light show commences, sending multicolored streaks across the air.

When Kanye steps on-stage, the crowd goes wild. Thousands of young fans surge to their feet, wave their arms in the air, and begin dancing along with the music. Kanye is dressed in a black jersey with his initials on the sleeve, leather pants, and sneakers. He looks good, as usual, and he's ready to bring the house down.

Lights: Kanye always puts on a dazzling show, complete with special lighting effects.

Amid all the visual excitement onstage, Kanye's own performance is riveting. He raps, he sings, and he dances, dazzling audiences with his signature musical style. People nod their heads along with the revolutionary rhythms, but his socially conscious lyrics also make people think about what the words mean.

When Kanye performs "Made in America," the house lights dim to create a solemn atmosphere. As audience members hold up lighters and cell phones in the darkness, videos of civil rights pioneers Martin Luther King Jr. and Malcolm X appear behind the performers.

Kanye West uses his music, lyrics, and beats to speak about the hard truths of the world and to tell what it means to be black in America. He sings about race, class, fame, politics, love, and even religion. He never backs down and never shies away from sharing his opinions. During one break in the concert, Jay-Z drapes an arm across Kanye's shoulders and shouts: "Atlanta, you are now looking at black excellence at its finest. Make some noise!"

Throughout the two-hour concert, Kanye shines. Even when he steps offstage, his presence and his messages continue to resonate with his fans. In the music industry, Kanye West is known as a quadruple threat because he works in four different roles: producer, rapper, beat maker, and record label executive. Tall, handsome, and always stylishly dressed, he is also a musical innovator, fashion icon, and all-around hip-hop rock star. His music comes from his soul, from his very self, yet the popularity of his albums makes it clear that his words have affected and inspired millions of people.

Birthplace: Kanye lived in Atlanta, Georgia *(pictured here in 1977, when Kanye was born)*, until the age of three. Then he and his mom moved to Chicago, Illinois.

Young Kanye

■■■■

Ray and Donda West were thrilled to be having a baby. Ray, a professional photographer, took dozens of pictures of Donda when she was pregnant. When their son was born on June 8, 1977, in Douglasville, Georgia (near Atlanta), Ray took many more pictures of the baby. He even photographed all the doctors and nurses who helped with the birth.

Ray and Donda hadn't picked out a name for the baby ahead of time, but they wanted their son to have an African name. In the 1970s, many black Americans were excited about connecting with their African roots. Ray and Donda wanted a name that would link their son to his distant ancestors.

Donda looked through a book of African names and chose Kanye Omari for her son. In Swahili, a language spoken in a wide region of eastern Africa, *kanye* means "only one." *Omari* means "wise man" in Swahili. Donda hoped Kanye would grow up to be special and brilliant, and she wanted him to be named accordingly.

Raised by Mom

A few months after Kanye was born, Ray opened a commercial photography studio in Atlanta. He, Donda, and baby Kanye lived in an apartment above the studio. Donda had a doctorate degree in English education from Alabama's Auburn University. Before and after Kanye

Parents: Kanye lived with his mother, Donda *(shown here in a 2005 photo)*, after his parents divorced. Even though they lived in different cities, Kanye remained close to his father, Ray *(shown here in a 2011 photo)*.

was born, she taught writing and English at colleges in Atlanta.

When Kanye was a baby, his parents began to grow apart. Just before Kanye turned one, his parents separated. Donda and Kanye moved to a new apartment in Atlanta. When Kanye was three years old, Donda and Ray divorced. Donda decided that she needed a fresh start. She accepted a teaching job at Chicago State University, a school with a mostly black student body.

Donda and Kanye moved to Chicago, Illinois. First, they lived in an apartment on the city's South Side. Then they moved to a house in a neighborhood called South Shore. Their home was close to the shores of Lake Michigan and close to Donda's job.

Kanye was an energetic and willful child. He had an unstoppable desire to speak his mind. Donda said that one of the biggest challenges in raising her son was figuring out "how to discipline Kanye without killing his spirit—how to support who he was and at the same time give him boundaries that would keep him within the parameters of what is appropriate." Kanye enjoyed testing those boundaries.

School Days

As an educator herself, Donda strove to ensure that Kanye had every opportunity to succeed in school. She enrolled him in Chicago's Vanderpoel Elementary School. The teachers and other staff at this school gave the students careful one-on-one attention. The student population was nearly 95 percent white. As one of the few African American students, Kanye stood out.

He thrived academically, but even as a young boy, Kanye was more interested in music than schoolwork. Every year the school held a talent show. Kanye entered for the first time in second grade. He dressed up like singer Stevie Wonder—in Stevie's trademark braids and sunglasses—and lip-synched to Stevie's song "I Just Called to Say I Love You." Kanye entered the show every year after that and usually won first prize.

At this time, hip-hop music was becoming popular. Kanye listened to hip-hop on the radio and sometimes made up his own raps. In addition to music, Kanye loved art. He was talented at drawing and painting and frequently won student art competitions.

Father Figures

Young Kanye did not have regular contact with his father, since they lived in distant cities. However, Kanye spent several summers in Atlanta with his father. He sometimes also visited on holidays. When Ray later moved to Maryland, Kanye visited him there too. The Christian faith was important to Ray West. In fact, he eventually switched careers, becoming a religious counselor. When Kanye visited, father and son attended church services on Sundays. Ray also taught Kanye about social justice. As a young man, Ray West had belonged to the Black Panther Party, a 1960s-era civil rights organization. Ray told Kanye about his work in the civil rights movement. He passed on his goals for racial equality to his son.

In addition to his father, Kanye had several other male role models. He was close to his uncles and other male relatives. Kanye grew particularly tight with his mother's father, Portwood Williams Sr., nicknamed Buddy. A former civil rights leader, Buddy gave Kanye a lot of encouragement. At least twice a year, Kanye and Donda traveled to Oklahoma City, Oklahoma, her hometown, to visit Buddy and other Williams relatives.

Donda West had several long-term boyfriends during Kanye's childhood. She was careful to put Kanye's needs first, though. She would introduce him to men she was dating only after getting to know them pretty well. She explained, "I didn't have a parade of men coming through. I had to be sure about the relationship (and it had to be a relationship, not just some fling) before I had a man meet my son." Donda hoped to meet a man who would become her husband and a good stepfather to Kanye.

When Kanye was ten years old, his mother became engaged to a man named Scotty. Scotty taught auto mechanics at a local school.

IN FOCUS

The Black Panthers

Before Kanye was born, his father belonged to the Black Panther Party, a radical community organizing group. The group formed during the civil rights movement, in 1966, in Oakland, California. The founders were young African Americans who had become frustrated with the slow pace of change toward racial equality in the United States. From Oakland, the Black Panthers soon spread to other major U.S. cities. The Panthers' mission was to stop police brutality against African Americans; to confront major social issues such as hunger, homelessness, and poverty; to promote quality education for black children; and to ensure a decent life for all Americans, regardless of color.

Justice: Kanye's father, Ray West, once belonged to the Black Panther Party. In this photo, Panthers stand outside a New York City courthouse in 1969.

He eventually moved into the house with Kanye and Donda. Scotty was a strong male role model for Kanye. He was strict and helped Donda keep Kanye in line. Scotty taught Kanye to do the right thing, including chores such as taking out the garbage. But sometimes the two butted heads.

Scotty and Donda never married. Their engagement ended in part because of Scotty's struggles with Kanye. Scotty believed in strong discipline, while Donda encouraged Kanye's independence and creativity, even if it meant not following every rule. One day Donda found Kanye crying at the kitchen table. Scotty had yelled at him about a small mistake. Kanye told his mom that he would rather go live with his father than live with Scotty any longer. He didn't really want to leave Chicago, and his mother knew it. So she ended the relationship with Scotty and continued raising Kanye on her own. Despite his conflict with Scotty, Kanye later told his mother that Scotty's influence had helped him become a responsible man. He even referred to Scotty as "my almost stepdad."

Living in China

When Kanye was ten, in 1987, Donda received a special opportunity to teach English in China for a year. She almost turned down the job because she did not want to leave Kanye behind. As it turned out, the teaching program allowed her to take Kanye along. The two traveled to Nanjing, China, where Donda taught at Nanjing University.

Kanye enrolled in a Chinese school. He didn't speak any Chinese, so the school placed him in first grade instead of fourth grade. He was much older than his classmates, but he was able to learn basic Chinese by doing writing and reading lessons with the younger students. The other students had never met an African American before, so Kanye stood out again, just as he had in his school in Chicago. But Kanye soon became popular with his classmates. Sometimes he put on breakdancing shows for them. He even charged admission to the shows. The other students paid him in coins and snacks.

Kanye spent time with the children of his mother's colleagues as well. These children came from various international locations, including Africa, Europe, and South America. Kanye and Donda also toured the region. They rode bikes on the crowded Nanjing streets and hiked in the countryside. When Donda had a six-week vacation from work, she and Kanye traveled to the Hong Kong region of China and then to Thailand, a nation in Southeast Asia. The trip was a grand adventure and a once-in-a-lifetime opportunity for both mother and son. After a year in China, they returned home to Chicago.

Finding His Own Style

In middle school, Kanye's grades began to decline. He spent most of his free time listening to music and making up raps. At the age of twelve, he paid twenty-five dollars to record a rap he called "Green Eggs and Ham" in a basement recording studio. With three friends, he put

Young rappers: In the early 1990s, the young rap duo Kriss Kross was popular. Kanye thought he could be even bigger than Kriss Kross.

together a rap group called Quadro Posse. They dressed in all black and won first place at a talent show at school.

In 1992 Kanye started at Polaris High School in Chicago. There, his grades slipped even more. He did well in art classes, but his real passion was music. He surrounded himself with only a few friends—other kids who were as excited about rap and music as he was. In addition to music, Kanye loved fashion. He often did his own laundry and even ironed his own clothes to make sure he looked sharp. He always wanted to wear the hottest shoes, such as expensive Air Jordan basketball shoes. For a while, he dressed in typical hip-hop style, in baggy pants and big T-shirts.

IN FOCUS

Recording Studio Terms

album: also called a record; a collection of musical compositions, sold together in one package, such as on a compact disc

beat: music played in the background behind rap lyrics, especially the sound of the drums

loop: a short segment of music played over and over again

mix: a blend of sounds (such as vocal tracks, drum rhythms, and instrumental music) created with a machine called a mixer

rap: rhythmic chanting or talking, usually performed to a background beat

record: also called an album; a collection of musical compositions, sold together in one package, usually as a compact disc. The term *record* can also refer to a vinyl phonographic disc (or LP).

record label: a company that produces and sells music

sample: a snippet of music from an existing song that other artists manipulate—for example, by speeding it up, slowing it down, or turning it into a loop

track: a single recorded song or other piece of music

Dreams Peeking Through

Kanye bought his first keyboard at the age of fourteen. He saved a whopping $500 toward the purchase, but that paid for only a portion of the instrument. His mother gave him the rest of the money as a Christmas present.

Kanye took odd and part-time jobs to support his music habit. He worked at the popular clothing chain Gap for a while. He also sold knives for a company called Cutco. For that job, he had to carry knives in a large wooden block and try to sell them to his friends and neighbors.

As soon as he had made enough money, Kanye bought turntables, a mixer, and a drum machine. As time went on, Kanye turned his bedroom into a music studio. He invited rapper and hip-hop friends to visit.

Education: Kanye West is seen in this 1995 high school yearbook photo.

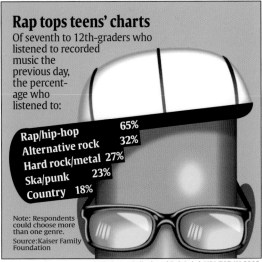

USA TODAY Snapshots®

Rap tops teens' charts

Of seventh to 12th-graders who listened to recorded music the previous day, the percentage who listened to:

Rap/hip-hop 65%
Alternative rock 32%
Hard rock/metal 27%
Ska/punk 23%
Country 18%

Note: Respondents could choose more than one genre.
Source: Kaiser Family Foundation

By Rebecca Pollack and Bob Laird, USA TODAY, 2005

IN F⊙CUS

Recording Equipment

drum machine: an electronic device that imitates the sound of various percussion instruments, such as drums and cymbals. Drum machines can be set to create a certain rhythm or beat.

keyboard: an electric version of a piano keyboard, with settings for creating different sound effects

mixer: a device that connects to electronic instruments, such as a keyboard, a drum machine, or an electric guitar. Music producers use mixers to regulate and balance sound levels coming from each instrument during a recording session.

turntable: a machine for playing vinyl phonographic discs (also called LPs). Modern turntables can be connected to mixers and other electronic equipment.

Beats ya'll: A producer needs a mixer *(center)*, a turntable *(left and right)*, and other equipment to create hip-hop beats.

Hip-Hop mentor: Common, shown here in 2003, taught Kanye about the music business.

They stayed in his room, churning out beats at all hours. Socializing with Kanye required going into the bedroom studio and trying to talk over the sound of the music.

Kanye's passion for hip-hop connected him with the thriving rap and hip-hop community in Chicago. He became friends with well-known local artists. He met Chicago rappers No I.D. (whose real name is Dion Wilson) and Common (real name Lonnie Lynn Jr., then known as Common Sense) in high school, and they served as mentors for him. He knew that he wanted to make his own name in the music business.

CHAPTER TWO

Giving it the college try: Kanye briefly attended Chicago State University, but he spent more time making music than he did studying.

Rise of a Producer

Kanye graduated from Polaris High School in 1995. Because of his artistic talent, he received a partial scholarship to attend the American Academy of Art in downtown Chicago. Kanye still lived at home with his mother and took the train downtown to school. Donda paid the portion of his tuition that wasn't covered by his scholarship.

The American Academy of Art offers degrees in commercial and fine art. Students there train for careers in illustration, graphic design, photography, and other artistic fields. After taking a few classes, Kanye decided he didn't want an art career. He left the American Academy of Art after only one semester because he wanted to devote more time to music.

Kanye's mother was not happy to learn that he was leaving school. As an educator, she firmly believed he needed a college degree to make a good living. She immediately enrolled him in the English Department at Chicago State University, where she taught. She wanted to oversee his education and help him get his diploma.

But Kanye rapidly lost interest in studying. He often skipped class and spent most of his time in the campus recording studios. His professors lost faith in him, saying Kanye was not a committed student. He completed two semesters at Chicago State before dropping out to pursue music full-time.

IN F⊕CUS

Respect for Mom

As a young man, Kanye liked playing his music for his mother. He knew she wanted to hear what he was working on. But he also worried that some of the lyrics might offend her. Sometimes he used rough language and curse words in his raps. Often he laid beats beneath someone else's lyrics, and some of those lyrics contained curse words too. Kanye didn't want his mother to hear all the bad words, so when he played songs for her that included cursing, he turned the volume way down during the roughest parts.

College Dropout

Donda was not happy when Kanye dropped out of Chicago State. She told him that if he was no longer a student, he'd have to pay rent to live at her house. She wanted him to understand that leaving school meant taking on adult responsibilities, such as earning money and managing your own finances.

Kanye took a job as a busboy at a Bob Evans restaurant. He showed up for the first day of work but quit without ever clearing a table. Next, he took a job as a telemarketer. In this job, he called people on the phone at home and tried to sell them insurance and other products. He liked to talk, so he stuck with telemarketing work for a while.

In his free time, Kanye steeped himself in Chicago's hip-hop community and culture. No I.D., whom Kanye had met in high school, took Kanye under his wing. No I.D. was considered the father of hip-hop in Chicago. He recognized Kanye's talent and helped Kanye become a full-fledged producer, recording tracks for other artists in his home studio.

Father of Chicago hip-hop: No I.D., seen here in 2009, helped Kanye become a professional producer.

IN F⊕CUS

Prank Caller

Once, while working as a telemarketer, Kanye prank-called his mother and gave her his normal sales pitch. She didn't realize that the smooth-talking young man on the other end of the phone was her own son. She didn't buy the product, but she listened for a while instead of hanging up, because she knew Kanye was doing the same kind of work as the young man on the phone. She wanted to be respectful to the caller. When Kanye revealed that he had made the call, they had a good laugh.

"I dropped out of school because I wasn't learning fast enough. . . . I learned better in real life."

—Kanye West to *Ebony* magazine, 2004

Kanye's Gift

From the beginning, Kanye injected a new style and rhythm into hip-hop. Hip-hop artists frequently use sampling, which involves pulling pieces from other musicians' recordings to use in the background of rap tracks. Kanye sampled extensively and from many different styles of music. Whereas other producers sampled mostly from hip-hop, Kanye used gospel and soul tracks. Since soul tended to be slow, Kanye sped up the music to a hipper tempo. He often mixed in rhythm and blues (R & B) samples from the 1960s and the 1970s. Many of the songs Kanye sampled were quite popular and familiar in their original forms. Kanye blended them with other music to create something fresh.

In his bedroom studio, Kanye created a unique, compelling sound.

USA TODAY Life SECTION D
LIFE.USATODAY.COM

August 12, 2003

Hip-Hop Entrepreneurs Get in Gear

<u>From the Pages of</u>
<u>USA TODAY</u>

Eve's got your back. So do Eminem, Beyoncé, 50 Cent and Nelly. They've got the rest of your body covered, too. They're just a few of the hip-hoppers who are infiltrating the fashion world with their own flashy clothing collections.

Of course, the upstarts will be facing stiff competition from Jennifer Lopez's established J. Lo line, P. Diddy's Sean John gear and Jay-Z's Rocawear garb. But that's not stopping Mariah Carey—not exactly known for wearing a surplus of garments—who is in talks to develop an accessory and jewelry line called Automatic Princess.

"It's this whole new idea of selling a lifestyle and putting a face on fashion, where before it was driven by faceless designers," says Barbara Coulon, vice president of trends at a Gen-X and Gen-Y research company called Youth Intelligence. "Now, someone's face and life is connected to it, so if you love Jay-Z, you can listen to his music, eat at his restaurant and wear his clothes."

Stepping into Jay-Z's sneakers is St. Louis hip-hop star Nelly, who already has two multiplatinum albums and a men's clothing line, Vokal, to his name. Now the Grammy nominee invites the ladies to Nellyville with his hip-hugging Apple Bottoms collection. "Hopefully in due time, we can get in with the Baby Phats (Kimora Lee Simmons' line) and the Rocawears," he says. "We look up to these lines."

So does Eve, the Philadelphia-based rapper who favors attention-grabbing Roberto Cavalli and Dolce & Gabbana outfits. She hopes her fans will steal her look by donning the denim skirts and slinky tops that are part of her Fetish line, in stores in September. Being a designing woman, she explains, is "about expressing my individuality."

It's exactly why her duds will be a hit, predicts *Seventeen* fashion editor Gigi Solis Schanen. "Kids see these musicians and want to be that person, because it's all about just being cool," Schanen says. "Eve and Beyoncé both have strong senses of style, and their clothes will be hot as long as they stay hot."

—Donna Freydkin

He made surprising choices, such as adding smooth melodies into harsher hip-hop beats. His thoughtful and broad-reaching approach to mixing, sampling, and beat making made him stand out.

Out of the House

Kanye's mother put up with the loud, pulsing music coming from her son's home studio for many years. Finally, she had had enough of the constant drumbeats and traffic of hip-hop artists in and out of her home. She told Kanye that he needed to either move out or find a separate studio.

Kanye chose to move out. He rented an apartment in Chicago's Beverly neighborhood and set up his studio in the small, second bedroom. By then, other rappers had started to take note of his talents. *Billboard* magazine later wrote, "Like so many others ... [Kanye] began as just another aspiring rapper with a boundless passion for hip-hop, albeit [although] a rapper with a Midas touch when it came to beatmaking. Indeed, it was his beatmaking prowess that got his foot in the industry door."

Beat making: Kanye sampled from the Jackson 5, shown here in 1972, as well as from other famous musicians.

Getting recognized: Rappers such as Jermaine Dupri, shown here in 1991, wanted to use Kanye's beats.

Soon after Kanye set up his new studio, well-known rapper Jermaine Dupri bought recordings of Kanye's beats to use in his own songs. Kanye got his first serious production job from the Chicago rapper Gravity, or Grav. Kanye mixed beats for Grav's record and worked with him on developing each track. Grav also paid Kanye $8,000 for some beats. This was the first big money Kanye made from his mixing business. "I knew then that Kanye was going to make it," Donda West said later.

Kanye's work with Grav brought him to the attention of rapper Jay-Z

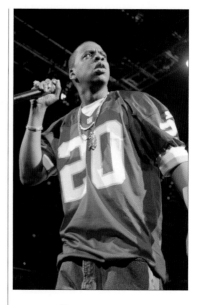

Roc-A-Fella: Kanye's career took off after he started working with Jay-Z, shown here in 1999.

(real name Shawn Carter), cofounder of Roc-A-Fella Records in New York. In 2000 Jay-Z hired Kanye to create some beats for his upcoming album *The Dynasty: Roc La Familia*, Kanye produced the song "This Can't Be Life" for the album. Kanye was thrilled. Getting Jay-Z's business meant that Kanye was beginning to hit the big time. He was ready to make the next step in his career. When his apartment lease ended, he decided to move to New York City.

IN F⊕CUS

Rap versus Hip-Hop

Sometimes the terms *rap* and *hip-hop* are used interchangeably, but their meanings are actually different. To rap means to speak in a rhythmic, poetic style. Hip-hop refers to a broader culture, including graffiti art, break dancing, certain styles of deejaying, certain clothing styles, and of course rap music.

Culture: Kids dance while a deejay spins hip-hop records.

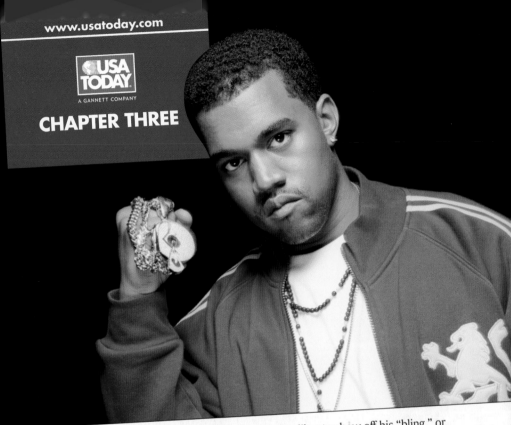

www.usatoday.com

CHAPTER THREE

Reaching for a goal: Like many other rappers, Kanye likes to show off his "bling," or flashy jewelry. He is pictured here in 2002.

Roc-A-Fella Days

Kanye moved to the New York City area in 2001. He wanted to pursue music producing full-time. His goal was to work with Roc-A-Fella studios, mixing and producing records for Jay-Z and other artists. He also had dreams of becoming a recording artist himself. He rented an apartment in Newark, New Jersey, within commuting distance of New York.

A Different Drummer

In the hip-hop world of the early 2000s, Kanye stood out. Many rap and hip-hop artists wore baggy jeans and other oversize clothing. Kanye had dressed that way for a while in high school. But by the time he came to New York, his style was more tailored and tidy. He preferred fitted polo shirts to baggy tees. He wore high-quality tailored pants instead of sagging jeans.

The first time Kanye walked into Roc-A-Fella studios to meet with Jay-Z and his business partners, they thought Kanye was wearing tailored clothing to make a joke. When they saw he was serious, they felt he would never fit in with the hip-hop world. But when they heard his beats, they realized that real talent existed beneath the preppy exterior.

Men behind the studio: Damon Dash *(left)*, Jay-Z *(center)*, and Kareem Burke *(right)*, the founders of Roc-A-Fella Records, pose with some of Jay-Z's gold records.

Jay-Z and Roc-A-Fella Studio

Jay-Z, Kanye's friend and mentor in the music business, was born Shawn Carter in Brooklyn, a borough (district) of New York City. Unlike Kanye, Jay-Z grew up in poverty. He was raised by a single mother in a housing project.

Jay-Z wanted to become a rapper. In New York, he met established hip-hop artists but couldn't get a record deal. In 1996, after being turned down by several major record labels, Jay-Z decided to start his own recording company, Roc-A-Fella Records. His friends Damon Dash and Kareem "Biggs" Burke worked with him to found the company. Roc-A-Fella's first album, Jay-Z's *Reasonable Doubt*, was released in 1997. The album did not make much money, but it did establish Roc-A-Fella as a new voice in the rap and hip-hop scene.

The record was also exciting enough to interest Def Jam Recordings, a larger record label, in what Jay-Z was doing. In 1997 Def Jam bought 50 percent of Roc-A-Fella Records. The Roc-A-Fella brand went on to expand into film production and a clothing line called Rocawear. In 2004 Def Jam bought the rest of Roc-A-Fella.

Kanye also stood out because of his middle-class upbringing. His parents were college educated, with good jobs. Kanye himself had graduated from high school and attended college for a time. He had grown up in a safe neighborhood. In contrast, many rappers came from poor backgrounds, unstable families, and crime-ridden neighborhoods. For example, Jay-Z had spent his childhood in an inner-city project, a housing development for poor families. His father had abandoned the family when Jay-Z was young. Jay-Z had not graduated from high school. He had dealt drugs and lived on the streets.

Jay-Z's music—and that of other rap and hip-hop artists—focused on life in the hood (inner-city neighborhood). Rappers spun lyrics about shootings, lootings, poverty, pain, and desperation. In fact, having "street cred" (credibility) was a huge part of making a name for oneself in hip-hop.

Kanye had no such rough-and-tumble background. Nevertheless, he had still made an emotional connection with rap and hip-hop music. He believed that hip-hop had space for a different perspective. While it was true that many hip-hop fans came from the hood and could identify with a "came from nothing and took some wrong turns" story like Jay-Z's, lots more came from stable backgrounds. Like Kanye, they liked the musical style, even though they didn't share the experiences of the rappers. Kanye wanted to be a rapper who spoke to those listeners.

 "We all grew up street guys who had to do whatever we had to do to get by. Then there's Kanye, who to my knowledge has never hustled [done dishonest work] a day in his life. I didn't see how it could work."

—Jay-Z, 2005

The Blueprint

With some hesitation, Jay-Z decided to take a chance on the strangely dressed, middle-class beat maker. Jay-Z signed Kanye as lead producer of his album *The Blueprint*. The album was a hit. It sold more than 420,000 copies the first week it was released, in September 2001. It included the standout singles "Takeover" and "Izzo (H.O.V.A)."

Kanye's beat-making style really shone on the album. "Takeover" sampled the classic rock group the Doors, and "Izzo (H.O.V.A)" sampled "I Want You Back" by the Jackson 5. Kanye popped to the center of attention in the hip-hop production world with this work.

September 26, 2001

Jay-Z's "Blueprint" more than music; Hip-hop artist is creating his own opportunities

<u>From the Pages of
USA TODAY</u> Jay-Z couldn't have risen from project streets to penthouse suites without a plan. On *The Blueprint*, his sixth album since 1996, he lays out how he capitalized on [took advantage of] his gift for rhyme to become a walking entertainment empire. With his company, Roc-A-Fella, he has rapidly become a hip-hop equivalent of the industrialist whose name he appropriated for the enterprise [John D. Rockefeller].

He used to wear the same clothes for days; now he makes millions selling clothes with his logo to the same people who keep his CDs moving out of the store. Court cases and critics haven't stopped him from becoming rap's most luminous star, and his gleeful indulgence in all things luxurious hasn't dampened the fervor with which his music is received on the streets. He has his share of detractors, but the way Jay-Z sees it, his story is one to emulate [imitate] rather than envy.

"I'm not in fancy cars trying to rub it in people's faces. I'm trying to serve as an example for them to see," Jay-Z says. "They can say, 'This guy is from 584 Flushing, Marcy Projects—and look where he's gotten to. I can definitely do it.' "

Not that any of his success came easy or overnight. Before Jay-Z, 30, ever popped Cristal champagne or wheeled his Bentley [a luxury car] through the Hamptons [wealthy communities on Long Island, New York], Shawn Carter hung out under streetlights selling drugs as a teenager. Fellow Brooklyn rapper Jaz brought him into the music business, but after watching Jaz's career fizzle, Carter became disenchanted with the rap game. Producer Clark Kent persuaded him to continue and introduced him to Damon Dash, who became his manager. Dash's friend Kareem "Biggs" Burke would soon join with them in a three-way partnership.

They spent nearly two years shopping Jay-Z's demo to record labels, but no one was interested. The trio formed Roc-A-Fella to put out an album before signing a distribution deal with Priority Records. They caught a break in early 1996, when "Ain't No Nigga," with newcomer Foxy Brown, became a surprise hit single off *The Nutty Professor* soundtrack. That summer, the autobiographical *Reasonable Doubt*, now considered a hip-hop classic, was released and went gold.

Jay-Z's success has proved to be a springboard for other Roc-A-Fella enterprises. The record label has successfully launched the careers of Memphis Bleek, DJ Clue, Amil and Beanie Sigel. Several other acts are waiting in the wings. The Hard Knock Life Tour, which made $18 million on 54 dates in 1999, was the biggest in hip-hop history. The Rocawear fashion line was introduced in 1999 and topped $100 million in sales in only 18 months. Roc-A-Fella Films has several movies in the works, including Mekhi Phifer's upcoming *Paid in Full*.

"Jay-Z is the Roy Jones Jr. of hip-hop," says Tonya Pendleton, music editor of BET. com. "They say that Roy Jones is the best boxer, pound for pound. I think Jay-Z is the best MC, pound for pound, but Roy doesn't have anyone to fight and Jay-Z doesn't have anybody to battle. He's a great writer, one of the few rappers you can listen to and understand every single word."

Dash says Jay-Z's inherent confidence appeals to both men and women, and relating to them on several levels keeps him from falling off. "He's very honest," Dash says. "Everything he talks about, he's done or experienced, and he does it in a way that's accessible to everybody."

The Blueprint's sound is sharper, more focused and more soulful than ever, in part because of the samples he uses. Snippets from Bobby Byrd, Bobby "Blue" Bland, David Ruffin, Al Green and Jackson 5 classics help give the album its feel, which takes him back to his childhood. "That was the music I heard when my mom was cleaning the kitchen with the windows open, and you could smell the Pine-Sol and Ajax all through the house," he says.

Now he's taking his own show on the road, but without the extravagant trappings of the Hard Knock Life Tour. The Blueprint Ballroom Tour, an 18-city club jaunt, puts him right in the midst of his supporters. He knows that while he's Big Pimpin' now and spending cheese, the streets are still watching.

"I'm still the same person," he says, tugging on his platinum-and-ice Roc-A-Fella medallion. "I been broke way, way, way longer than I've been rich. Five years ain't going to change my whole life."

—Steve Jones

The success of Jay-Z's album helped Kanye become known as a talented music producer. He was soon producing records for other Roc-A-Fella stars, including rapper Ludacris and singer Beyoncé. But he was not widely known outside of production circles.

Frustrated

Kanye loved producing. He loved being in the studio, behind the scenes. But he also dreamed of standing on the other side of the microphone. He wrote raps of his own, applied his own beats,

Partners: Kanye hangs out with Jay-Z *(right)*backstage at the 2004 MTV Video Music Awards in Miami, Florida.

and recorded demo (demonstration) tracks to show off his skills. He hoped he could get a record label to sign him as a solo artist. But although everyone recognized Kanye's talent as a beat maker and a producer, no one seemed interested in signing him as a rapper.

In 2002 Kanye rapped as a guest artist for Jay-Z's next album, *The Blueprint 2: The Gift and the Curse*. Kanye hoped this experience would bring him closer to a record deal. But as he waited for somebody to take a chance on him, he grew frustrated and impatient. "Whether it was because I didn't have a larger-than-life persona, or I was perceived

The Roc-A-Fella family: Damon Dash, wearing a Rocawear jacket, consults with Kanye. In 2002 Roc-A-Fella gave Kanye a deal to make his own record.

as the guy who made beats, I was disrespected as a rapper," he said.

Finally, in the summer of 2002, Roc-A-Fella gave Kanye the record deal he had been waiting for. As Kanye began preparing to make his own record, he continued working as a producer for other rappers.

Near-Fatal Crash
In October 2002, Kanye traveled to Los Angeles, California, to help produce a record for rappers Beanie Sigel and Peedi Crakk. He stayed at a hotel called W Los Angeles. While driving home from a late-night recording session, he fell asleep at the wheel. He lost control of the car and ended up in a head-on collision with another vehicle.

Although disoriented and confused, from the wreckage of the car, Kanye used his cell phone to call his girlfriend, Sumeke Rainey. She called Donda, who then called Kanye. She talked to him only briefly before the police and paramedics arrived.

The paramedics had to use power tools to cut Kanye out of the smashed vehicle. They rushed him to the hospital. Kanye's injuries were severe. His jaw was broken in three places. Bones in his nose were also broken. The driver of the car that Kanye had hit was also badly injured. He had two broken legs.

Doctors performed plastic surgery on Kanye's damaged face. To repair the broken jaw, they had to wire it shut.

Donda flew from Chicago to Los Angeles to care for Kanye after the accident. They both stayed in the W Los Angeles for several weeks. With his jaw wired shut, Kanye could eat only through a straw. He lived on a diet of broth, juice, smoothies, and milk shakes—only foods he could suck through the narrow gaps between the wires that held his jaw shut.

Kanye did not let his injuries keep him down. If anything, nearly losing his life made him dig into his work even deeper. He wanted to make a name for himself. He did not want to keep his dreams on hold any longer.

Hard work: Kanye, shown here in New York in 2004, also worked in Los Angeles.

"Through the Wire"

Instead of viewing the car accident as a setback, Kanye used it as a stepping-stone. He used it as inspiration for a new song, "Through the Wire" (2003), which told about his accident and his recovery.

He called the staff at Roc-A-Fella and asked them to send a drum machine to his hotel suite. Only three weeks after the accident, he turned the suite into a music studio and started recording "Through the Wire." The song sampled singer Chaka Khan's 1984 hit "Through the Fire." Kanye liked the connection between Khan's song title and his own.

Despite pain in his mouth, he recorded the song while his jaw was still wired shut. He later told *Ebony* magazine: "I feel like the [recording work] was my medicine. It would take my mind away from the pain—away from the dental appointments, from my teeth killing me, from my mouth being wired shut, from the fact that I looked like I just fought [heavyweight boxer] Mike Tyson."

The lyrics were a bit muffled, but when the song came out on the radio in 2003 as a single—a song released by itself, without an album— Kanye began to gain a following. Later, he joked that he had needed a sensational spark like a car accident to get his solo career going. He explained that his life-threatening experience had finally given him the street cred he needed to succeed. "Death is the best thing that can ever happen to a rapper," he said. "Almost dying isn't bad either."

Giving Back

The production of Kanye's first album continued through 2003. With his record deal and the popularity of "Through the Wire," he was finally achieving some fame and financial success as a rapper. So he decided to give something back. He wanted to reach out to communities in need, especially black youth. That year, Kanye founded a charitable organization called the Kanye West Foundation. His mother, Donda, set up the charity. She also became its manager. (The foundation closed its doors in 2011.)

A Grand Debut

After several delays, Roc-A-Fella released *The College Dropout* in the fall of 2004. Kanye was thrilled when the record finally arrived in stores. His mother was also thrilled. She went to a music store, bought ten copies of the CD, pointed to the cover, and proudly told the salesclerk, "This is my son's."

Helping children: Kanye poses with kids in Chicago from Students Helping Our World (SHOW), a group that motivates high school students to improve their grades and attendance.

IN F⊕CUS

Dropout Bear

The cover of *The College Dropout* features Kanye sitting on gym bleachers wearing a school mascot costume, a bear. The furry creature, called the Dropout Bear, also appears on the album covers for Kanye's *Late Registration* and *Graduation*.

Album mascot: Kanye and the Dropout Bear appeared on MTV's *Total Request Live* television show in 2004.

December 23, 2003

The Common Man's Hip-Hop; on the Verge?? Kanye West

From the Pages of USA TODAY

Personal: 26-year-old Chicago native Kanye West is one of hip-hop's premier producers, now emerging as an artist. He nearly died in a car crash in Los Angeles in October 2002, just a few months after signing as an artist with Roc-A-Fella Records. It was during that time—with his broken jaw wired shut—that he recorded current hit "Through the Wire," a deeply personal, sometimes witty account of the experience. "Who would have thought that that would be a hit single?" he says.

Buzz: More than a dozen media outlets have named his *College Dropout*, which is due February 3, as one of the most anticipated albums of 2004. In addition to "Through the Wire," he's also featured on Twista's "Slow Jamz," giving him the two hottest singles on the Nielsen SoundScan national radio chart earlier this month. The album features appearances by several of West's past collaborators, including Jay-Z, Mos Def, Freeway, Ludacris and Twista.

Kanye's album debuted to great praise from music reviewers. It sold 440,000 copies in the first week. Listeners admired Kanye's blend of socially conscious lyrics and hot, of-the-moment beats. "Through the Wire" was the album's headline song. Another song, "All Falls Down," dealt with materialism—that is, people's preoccupation with buying expensive cars, clothes, and watches.

"I knew that in thirty-one years of teaching, I had not impacted young people the way this single record would," Donda West said

History: West began making beats when he was 14. His big break came when he was introduced to Jay-Z, who used a West beat on Beanie Sigel's *The Truth* in 2000. He has become one of Jay-Z's favorite producers, working on "Izzo (H.O.V.A.)," "'03 Bonnie and Clyde" and "Encore"—and has provided soulful beats for Alicia Keys ("You Don't Know My Name"), Scarface ("Guess Who's Back"), Talib Kweli ("Get By"), Ludacris ("Stand Up") and many others.

Getting the runaround: West says he has been rapping since he was in third grade, but he could never persuade anybody to give him a shot. Everyone, it seems, was always more impressed with his production abilities. "Some people tell me that I rap so much better than when they had a chance to sign me. I'll play them a song and they'll say, 'See,' but it will be something I recorded a long time ago. But that's cool. The tables have been turned."

Rapping to a different beat: Other artists have spun tales about gangsters, drugs, sex, clubbing and the like. But West says he represents the common man. "It's more like the person who works at the Gap but still likes nice clothes, or the guy with a regular job and a car payment who was finally able to afford some rims by the summer."

Overflowing confidence: "One advantage I have is that all my beats are phenomenal. I gave up a couple (including the one for Lucifer on Jay-Z's *The Black Album*), but for the most part, I think it's a classic album."

—Steve Jones

about her son's debut album. "It would also touch the old and everyone in between. To me, it was hip-hop and gospel, pop and blues all at the same time."

Some people criticized the name of the album, *The College Dropout*. Critics said the album's name glorified the idea of dropping out of school. In response, Kanye insisted that he was just talking about what had happened in his own life. He was not trying to encourage anyone to drop out.

Going platinum: *The College Dropout* went platinum—sold one million copies—in just eight weeks after its release. At a ceremony in San Francisco, California, in 2004, the Recording Industry Association of America presented Kanye with a platinum-plated copy of the record, mounted in a frame.

"Jesus Walks"

One of the songs on *The College Dropout*, "Jesus Walks," talks about having faith in Jesus, the central holy figure of Christianity. The song's message is uplifting, but it also allows room for uncertainty and questioning about God and religion.

Some Christians criticized the song, which mixes the harsh language of hip-hop with religious references. The video for the song also included disturbing images of white prison guards abusing black prisoners, drug smuggling, and a member of the Ku Klux Klan (a white terrorist group) burning a cross to threaten and frighten black people.

February 10, 2005

Kanye West Runs Away with "Jesus Walks"

<u>From the Pages of
USA TODAY</u>

Three years ago, when Kanye West was trying to get a record deal, the then-rising producer was told that "Jesus Walks" would never get any radio play.

It turned out to be the biggest hit from his *College Dropout* debut. The rapper, 27, will perform it Sunday at the 47th Grammy Awards in L.A. with his R&B protégé John Legend and gospel titans Mavis Staples and the Blind Boys of Alabama.

West has the most nominations with 10, including two for "Jesus Walks": song and rap song. The frustrations he encountered trying to sell the song show up in its second verse: "So here go my single, dog, radio needs this/They say you can rap about anything except for Jesus/That means guns, sex, lies, videotapes/But if I talk about God, my record won't get played, huh?"

"It was never a problem once it came out," says West, who has produced hits for the likes of Jay-Z, Alicia Keys, Janet Jackson and Ludacris. "All I did was use reverse psychology. It was a way of calling out people who didn't want to play it without pointing fingers at anybody."

West says he knew all along that he would prove naysayers wrong with his album, which sold 2.5 million copies. He went against the gangster grain and dealt more with human frailties. What he didn't expect was all the accolades [praise].

"I thought that people would like it a lot, and the songs would blow up, and people would buy the album," says West, who also drew praise for his performances last summer on Usher's Truth Tour. "But the Grammy nominations were just overwhelming. I remember as a little kid dreaming that I would get a chance to be at the Grammys. I never thought I would get 10 (nominations). I would have been happy with just one. The Grammys really open up doors. It makes you official."

West won't be resting on his laurels. He is finishing his follow-up album, *Late Registration*, which he hopes to have out in late March or April.

—Steve Jones

Kanye said that he intended the song to be a personal reflection on religion, as well as a bridge between the rap-listening and churchgoing sides of the black community. Though many people participate in both aspects of black culture, some churchgoers view rap as negative and sinful because rap often glorifies casual sex, illegal drugs, and gun violence.

Kanye said that hip-hop culture and church did not have to be at odds with one another. He also said that an entire genre of music should not be demonized because some artists chose to express themselves in ways that did not mesh with Christianity. He wanted to show that rap and hip-hop could actually be used to spread a message of love, faith, and spiritual exploration.

Working together: Kanye used his skills as a producer to help other artists make great records. One of his collaborators was Alicia Keys, shown here with Kanye in 2004.

Collaborations

While Kanye began to enjoy solo success, he was still producing hit songs for other artists. Two songs he produced in 2003, "Stand Up" by Ludacris and "You Don't Know My Name" by Alicia Keys, became number one hits

On tour: Usher *(left)* and Kanye perform to a sold-out crowd at the Staples Center in Los Angeles during the Truth Tour in 2004.

around the time Kanye's first album came out. "Slow Jamz," a collaboration with Twista, became Kanye's first number one hit as a rapper. "Slow Jamz" appeared on Twista's album *Kamikaze* (2004) and was also included on Kanye's *The College Dropout*.

In the summer of 2004, the famous R & B singer Usher invited Kanye to participate in a national concert series, the Truth Tour, to promote Usher's 2004 album *Confessions*. From August to October that year, Kanye served as the opening act for Usher, performing songs from his debut album and introducing himself to Usher's fans.

While touring with Usher, Kanye worked with an organization called Youth Movement Records, based in Oakland, California. The group brought award-winning musicians and other famous artists to schools to meet with underprivileged students. Kanye visited students in Oakland and encouraged them to set ambitious goals and do everything they could to make them come true. The kids were all interested in making music, and Kanye knew it was good for them to meet a successful musician. He hoped to inspire them to believe that they could succeed in music too.

Best New Artist?

Every year, the ABC television network broadcasts the American Music Awards, which honor outstanding musicians. In the fall of 2004, Kanye was nominated for the AMA best new artist award. He and the other nominees attended the awards ceremony in Los Angeles on November 14, 2004.

Sitting in the audience for the announcement of the best new artist award, Kanye hoped his name would be called, but country singer Gretchen Wilson won the award instead. When he heard her name called instead of his, Kanye stormed the stage and then left the auditorium in a huff. Leaving was his way of protesting the results. "I felt like I was definitely robbed," he

Upset: Kanye comes onstage, uninvited, as Gretchen Wilson *(right)* accepts the best new artist award at the American Music Awards in 2004. Kanye thought he deserved to win.

IN F⊕CUS

Billboard Magazine

Billboard is a highly influential magazine in the music world. The magazine gives awards and tracks the best-selling songs and albums on a weekly, monthly, and annual basis. Every musician dreams of seeing his or her name as a number one on the *Billboard* music charts.

told reporters. "I was the best new artist this year." He criticized the show's voting process and claimed he'd never return to the American Music Awards.

"Kanye hates to lose. He hates coming in second. It's just the way he's wired," said his mother after the incident. Not only did Kanye hate to lose, he constantly expected to win. After his

Angelic: Kanye performs "Jesus Walks" at the Grammy Awards in 2005.

Winning moment: Kanye accepts his Grammy for best rap song, "Jesus Walks," at the 2005 awards ceremony.

ungracious loss at the American Music Awards, public attention was on Kanye as the Grammy Awards approached the following spring. The Grammys are the most prestigious music awards in the United States.

Kanye earned ten Grammy nominations for the 2005 show. Held in Los Angeles on February 13, the event was televised nationally. All the biggest stars in music were invited. The dress code for the show was black tie, which meant that men wore tuxedos and women wore evening gowns. Reporters, photographers, and fans lined the red carpet that led from the parking lot to the theater entrance, eagerly waiting for celebrities to get out of their cars and walk inside.

Kanye knew that people were watching him closely, wondering if he would again walk out of the auditorium if he didn't win an award. But this time he did win. "Jesus Walks" won the award for best rap song, and *The College Dropout* won for best rap album. "A lot of people were wondering what I was going to do if I didn't win anything," he said when he accepted the second award. "I guess we'll never know."

Kanye was starting to earn a reputation for arrogance. But he was also earning great acclaim. In fact, in 2005 he made *Time* magazine's list of the "One Hundred Most Influential People in the World." With millions of dollars flowing into his bank account, Kanye bought an expensive home in an upscale neighborhood in Los Angeles. He had finally made it to the big time.

In front of a crowd: Kanye performs at a Super Bowl concert series in Jacksonville, Florida, in 2005.

Star Power

■■■■■

As his solo career gained speed, Kanye kept on producing tracks and albums for other talented artists. Jay-Z continued to use Kanye's talent behind the scenes. Well-established performers (Janet Jackson) and up-and-coming singers (Beyoncé) alike used Kanye's beats. Time and again, the tracks he produced turned into chart-topping hits.

Meanwhile, Kanye poured everything he had, creatively and financially, into a second album, *Late Registration*. He brought in huge names, including Jay-Z, actor Jamie Foxx, singers Nas and Brandy, and Maroon 5's Adam Levine, as guest artists on the album. He paid large-scale bands and orchestras to provide backup music. The production costs on *Late Registration* exceeded $2 million.

Collaborators: *Top:* Beyoncé made hit records using Kanye's beats. *Above:* Kanye sings with Adam Levine of Maroon 5 at a concert to celebrate the opening of the 2005 National Football League season. Adam Levine was a guest artist on *Late Registration*.

LIFE.USATODAY.COM

August 30, 2005

Kanye West's "Registration" Is Right on Time; Sophomore Album Scores a Solid "A"

From the Pages of
USA TODAY

Kanye West may have been The College Dropout on his first album, but he keeps acing his final exams. With *Late Registration* (**** out of four), he breezes through his latest test by crafting a sophomore album that is deeper and richer than his multiplatinum, Grammy-winning debut.

He could have been excused for sticking with what works—most artists do—but he took his follow-up as an opportunity to grow. With co-producer Jon Brion (Aimee Mann, Fiona Apple), West expands his sonic [sound] offerings beyond his usual speeded-up R&B samples with a broader array of instrumentation to serve as a backdrop for his improving lyricism.

And while at times he comes off as being full of himself, and he's certainly full of contradictions, he never fails to be engaging and entertaining. West has taken hip-hop in a fresh direction by exploring ideas beyond the thug lifestyle and attitude. He also has pushed the envelope for production with his choices in sounds and collaborators.

On "Diamonds of Sierra Leone," he ties the civil war in that country to the diamond and drug trades. In the same song, he chides himself for his tantrum last year after losing at the American Music Awards.

The humorous "Golddigger" features a Ray Charles sample along with Jamie Foxx ad-libbing as Ray Charles while West goes on about women who will burn a hole in a man's pocket.

A snarling "Game" helps drive home . . . theories about government conspiracies against the black community, and Maroon 5 singer Adam Levine's smooth tenor punctuates the introspective "Heard 'Em Say." "Roses" criticizes the lack of universal health care in the USA through a poignant story about his ailing grandmother. On

Sophmore album: The *Late Registration* CD features a picture of the Dropout Bear.

"Addiction," West addresses his own inner conflicts and asks, "Why is it that everything they say is so bad makes me feel so good?"

West's sense of irony finds his Def Jam/Roc-A-Fella boss Jay-Z rhyming on the "Diamonds" remix, which is followed immediately by Jay-Z's one-time antagonist [rival] Nas on "We Major." It's refreshing to see an artist choosing to push himself beyond his usual boundaries and giving listeners more than they'd expect. West has managed to be adventurous without going so far afield that you can't—or wouldn't want to—follow where he's leading. With two albums to go in what he has dubbed his college series, he could have a few more master classes on his schedule.

—Steve Jones

Kicking back between hits: Kanye works on recording *Late Registration* in 2005.

Rap with a Message

Late Registration debuted in 2005. Featuring Kanye's magic combination of beats and samples, the record soon reached the top of the charts. Several songs on the album—"Diamonds from Sierra Leone," "Gold Digger," "Heard 'Em Say," and "Touch the Sky"— became hit singles.

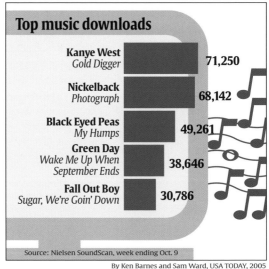

USA TODAY Snapshots®

Top music downloads

Artist / Song	Downloads
Kanye West *Gold Digger*	71,250
Nickelback *Photograph*	68,142
Black Eyed Peas *My Humps*	49,261
Green Day *Wake Me Up When September Ends*	38,646
Fall Out Boy *Sugar, We're Goin' Down*	30,786

Source: Nielsen SoundScan, week ending Oct. 9

By Ken Barnes and Sam Ward, USA TODAY, 2005

Late Registration featured Kanye's particular flair for social commentary. In "Gold Digger," for instance, he criticizes women who look for wealthy boyfriends instead of dating working-class men. "Diamonds from Sierra Leone" sheds light on the blood diamond trade in West Africa, where money from the sale of African-mined diamonds is used to fund war and criminal activity.

But Kanye also balanced out the social commentary with humor and lighter material. He knew that if the subject matter was too heavy, the record would not climb the charts. "I want to mix a bit of what appeals to people's bad sides with a bit of what appeals to their good sides," he said.

The album hit stores in August 2005 and sold more than 1.5 million copies the first week. *Rolling Stone* magazine gave *Late Registration* five stars out of five. Reviewer Rob Sheffield wrote that the album was "an undeniable triumph."

Heavy material: Diamond miners in Sierra Leone toil for low pay. Kanye's song "Diamonds from Sierra Leone" focuses on the corrupt African diamond industry.

September 28, 2006

Music, film open eyes to war in Sierra Leone

<u>From the Pages of</u>
<u>USA TODAY</u>

Two music projects offer views of Sierra Leone's civil war through the eyes of some of the people who experienced it. Sierra Leone's Refugee All Stars, already the subject of an award-winning documentary this year and a U.S. summer tour, released *Living Like a Refugee* this week. The album features music recorded by the 11-member band during the musicians' time in exile and after they returned home. They'll return to North America starting October 21 in Atlanta for a 19-date tour. In December, VH1 is scheduled to air *Bling: A Planet Rock*, a documentary that traces hip-hop's fascination with diamonds and the illegal gem trade that helped fuel the war. Director Raquel Cepeda goes to Sierra Leone with reggaeton's Tego Calderon and rappers Paul Wall and Raekwon to see the devastation firsthand.

The war between the government and rebel forces over control of the country's diamond trade lasted from 1991 to 2002, killing tens of thousands of people and displacing 2 million. Much of the country remains without drinking water and electricity.

Refugee All Stars founder Reuben M. Koroma gathered his band in Guinea refugee camps after fleeing the capital city, Freetown, in 1999. The band was discovered by first-time filmmakers Zach Niles and Banker White, who followed them for three years.

Koroma, who witnessed the slaughter of several family members, turned to music to ease his pain. "I used music as a therapy, and I noticed that anytime I'd strum my guitar, most of the refugees would gather around me," he said from his home in Sierra Leone.

The band went from playing in the camps to performing before 75,000 people at this summer's Bonnaroo Festival in Tennessee. "I hope that people will learn about the situation in our country," Koroma says. "I hope that it brings a positive change to the world."

Cepeda wishes the same for her film, which she hopes gets hip-hop artists and fans to think about the diamonds they wear. "I hope that by seeing rappers travel, it would encourage young people to see how people live around the world so that they can become a different type of American—one not so insulated and kind of selfish," says Cepeda, who co-produced the film with Article 19 Films, VH1 and the United Nations Development Program.

Fighting injustice: Kanye West and other artists, such as Sierra Leone's Refugee All-Stars, have used music to call attention to injustice in Sierra Leone.

Houston rapper Wall, a professional jeweler who is known for his custom diamond-studded teeth grills, says he had never heard of the country until last year's Kanye West single "Diamonds from Sierra Leone." Wall says he met miners who earned $2 for each diamond they found. He says he presumes the diamonds he uses are legal but says he feels obligated to spread the word about what he saw.

—Steve Jones

The success of *Late Registration* merely added fuel to Kanye's self-confidence. He didn't even wait to be nominated for awards before stating that he deserved to win them. In an interview with MTV News, he declared that he would have "a real problem" if his record weren't named album of the year at all the major music award shows. Kanye also said he deserved to win because he had spent so much money producing his hit songs.

Beautiful mother: At the 2006 Grammy Awards, Kanye celebrated with his mother, Donda.

Ladies' Man and Mama's Boy

Like many rock stars, Kanye usually had a beautiful woman on his arm. He dated Sumeke Rainey for several years. His next love was fashion designer Alexis Phifer. They were even engaged for a while. But no matter whom he was dating, the most important woman in his life remained his mother. When Kanye finally made it big in the music business, Donda West quit her teaching job. She became Kanye's manager and also ran the Kanye West Foundation. When Kanye moved to Los Angeles, Donda moved there too.

Sometimes friends gave Kanye flak for his close connection with his mother. They called him a mama's boy. But Kanye and his mother were both proud of the relationship they shared. "My mama's my best friend. I talk to her every day," he explained.

Help for Sierra Leone

With his song "Diamonds from Sierra Leone," Kanye wanted to bring attention to the vicious diamond trade in West Africa. The money from diamonds mined in Sierra Leone often goes to fund war crimes, terrorism, and other atrocities.

When music video casting director Tiffany Persons heard Kanye's song, she thought he might be able to help the people of Sierra Leone even more. Persons had visited the West African nation to make a documentary film. In a village there, she saw the terrible conditions endured by workers in the nation's diamond mines. The miners earned only $1.33 and a cup of rice per day. They could not afford to feed their families. The village school was a falling-down building without a roof.

Persons started a charity called Shine on Sierra Leone to restore the school and to help the people of Sierra Leone in many other ways. When Donda and Kanye heard about the charity, they knew they wanted to help. The Kanye West Foundation made a generous donation to Shine on Sierra Leone.

A New Kind of Rapper

Many people criticize rap music for disrespecting women. Some rap songs use ugly words to describe women. Many rap songs paint women as merely sexual objects. Kanye knew many rappers who included such mean-spirited lyrics in their songs. They tried to be macho he-men. Putting down women was part of their tough-guy images.

Kanye could be hard on women too. His song "Gold Digger" takes a swipe at women who would rather date wealthy men than poor ones. In other songs, Kanye boasts about his sexual conquests. At the same time, Kanye did not act supermacho the way other rappers did. He was not afraid to rap about his own fears, frustrations, and failures. When he rapped about women, he often talked about love and relationships.

USA TODAY
Life
SECTION D

LIFE.USATODAY.COM

August 22, 2005

West Hopes to Register with Musical Daring; Producer Brings "Cinematic" Sound

From the Pages of
USA TODAY

Kanye West is certain his *Late Registration* will ace the sales test Friday. What he wants to know is whether it will stand the test of time.

The never-shy producer/rapper says his newest album is sonically superior to last year's Grammy-winning debut, *The College Dropout*, and stacks up well against other classic albums.

"Music hasn't been taken this far in years—since Stevie (Wonder) did it. Since Prince did it," says West, 27, who enlisted Fiona Apple producer Jon Brion to help him go in a different direction.

West has had a good year. He won three Grammys and delivered a show-stopping "Jesus Walks" on the awards program, and he produced two of 2005's most acclaimed albums—John Legend's *Get Lifted* and Common's *Be*. But the real question was what would he do for an encore to *Dropout*.

In addition to putting down women, some rappers put down gay people—particularly gay men. Kanye has a gay cousin in Oklahoma City whom he loves deeply. He realized that all the gay bashing in rap music was wrong. In August 2005, at an MTV special called "All Eyes on Kanye West," Kanye decided to take a stand. He said: "It's not just hip-hop, but America just discriminates against gay people. I want to just come on TV, and just tell my rappers, just tell my friends, "Yo,

On *Registration*, he talks about everything from politics to partying, and guest artists include Maroon 5's Adam Levine, Jamie Foxx, Common, The Game, Brandy, Nas, Cam'Ron and Jay-Z. His most daring move was bringing in multi-instrumentalist Brion, who had scored such movies as *Eternal Sunshine of the Spotless Mind* and *Punch-Drunk Love*.

West, who came into prominence four years ago with Jay-Z's groundbreaking *The Blueprint*, was seeking a new plateau in production. "Picture me, someone who likes cinematic-sounding stuff, having someone who actually scores movies to help produce the album," West says.

Brion says that although some might find their pairing odd, he and West shared a seriousness about making records and "a total obsession with lyrics." Brion's skill with orchestras and with such instruments as vibraphones and marimbas gave West a much broader spectrum of sounds to work with.

West showed a lot of courage, Brion says, by stepping out on an artistic ledge. "If ever there was a time not to (mess) with the formula, this would be it," Brion says. "But he's fearless. A lot of people have a governor on themselves, usually peer pressure or fear of not being liked. This is a guy that is truly living by his tastes and his beliefs."

The result is "only the future of music itself," West says, laughing. "Only a Dr. Dre or a Pharrell (Williams) could even fathom accomplishing something like this, and they do it in their own way."

West, who likens himself to the Philadelphia Eagles' brash Terrell Owens, makes no apologies for talking smack. "Are you supposed to be humble?" he says. "Honestly. If you've got a whole crowd of people singing your song and you've got one critic saying this song is OK, well, you know you're right."

—Steve Jones

stop it." After that statement, Kanye received a flood of e-mails and phone calls from both gay and straight people, thanking him for taking a stand against discrimination.

Working together: Mike Myers (*left*) and Kanye chat in 2005. Earlier in the year, the two appeared together at a fund-raiser for victims of Hurricane Katrina where Kanye spoke out against President George Bush's slow response to the disaster.

All Eyes on Kanye

■■■■

In 2005 a massive hurricane developed in the Gulf of Mexico, south of the United States. Named Hurricane Katrina, the storm made landfall on August 29, smashing into the Gulf Coast from Florida across to Texas. The hurricane brought massive waves and high winds to coastal areas.

Some of the worst damage occurred in New Orleans, Louisiana. There, levees that had been built to prevent the city from flooding during big rainstorms,

Escaping the rising water: As floodwaters rose in the streets of New Orleans, Louisiana, after the 2005 hurricane, residents sought safety on roofs.

broke. Water rushed over these massive walls and flooded the city.

City officials had urged citizens to leave New Orleans in the days before the storm, but not everyone was able to travel. Many poor people didn't have cars or other ways to get out of town. Many of those left behind were African Americans. Some of them climbed into their attics or onto their roofs to escape the rising floodwaters in the streets below.

In the days following the hurricane, the U.S. government's rescue efforts were slow and poorly coordinated. Rescuers did not get to everyone in time. Several thousand people drowned in their houses and in the streets of New Orleans.

On September 2, along with other performers, Kanye took part in a televised concert to raise money to help hurricane victims. During one portion of the broadcast, Kanye and comedian Mike Myers addressed television viewers, asking them to call in with donations. Kanye spoke about the agony of seeing people stranded in New Orleans, without food, waiting for help that was coming too late or not coming at all. He also talked about a double standard used by the media: When black people stranded in New Orleans broke into stores to get food, the media said they were "looting"— committing a crime. When white people did the same thing, reporters said they were simply "getting food." After explaining this double standard, Kanye blurted out, "[President] George Bush doesn't care about black people."

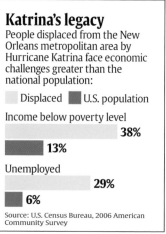

Katrina's legacy

People displaced from the New Orleans metropolitan area by Hurricane Katrina face economic challenges greater than the national population:

☐ Displaced ■ U.S. population

Income below poverty level

38%

13%

Unemployed

29%

6%

Source: U.S. Census Bureau, 2006 American Community Survey

By Veronica Salazar, USA TODAY, 2007

Kanye's on-air outburst added fuel to a fire that was already burning: many Americans, particularly people of color, were upset with the

President on location: Kanye lashed out at President Bush, here touring Biloxi, Mississippi, after the hurricane in 2005. Kanye suggested the president was racist.

U.S. government's slow response in the wake of the hurricane. They argued that President Bush had failed to help those most in need—the poorest citizens of New Orleans.

A lot of people applauded Kanye's blunt comments about President Bush. Others felt he was out of line for criticizing the nation's president on live television. President Bush himself said that he was disgusted by Kanye's comments. He said he was not a racist.

Kanye later issued a public apology to President Bush. In a televised interview with TV anchor Matt Lauer, Kanye said, "I would tell George Bush [that] in my moment of frustration, I didn't have the grounds to call him a racist." But the apology did not get Kanye out of hot water. Some people who had agreed with his initial statement became angry at him for taking it back.

Meanwhile, Kanye did whatever he could to help the people of New Orleans. He made a big donation to help people put their lives and homes back together. He and his mother also visited the Astrodome in Houston, Texas. This sports stadium served as a temporary home for hundreds of mostly poor black people whose houses had been flooded in New Orleans. Kanye gave out gifts to the children there and spoke with people one on one. Many of them thanked him for his blunt words about President Bush.

Kanye as Messiah?

Just as the controversy over his George Bush remark was dying down, Kanye stirred up a new controversy. In February 2006, he posed for pictures in *Rolling Stone* magazine. The cover of the issue showed Kanye styled as Jesus Christ, wearing a crown of thorns. According to Christian beliefs, Jesus was made to wear a crown of thorns before being killed by people who did not believe he was a religious savior. The article inside the magazine was titled "The Passion of Kanye West." The term *passion* often refers to the sufferings of Jesus before his death. Both the title of the article and the cover photo referenced Kanye's popular single "Jesus Walks."

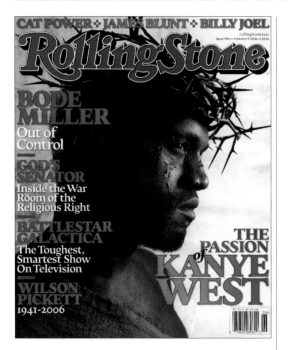

Passionate cover: When Kanye posed in a crown of thorns on the cover of *Rolling Stone* in 2006, some people felt he was mocking religion.

Not surprisingly, the cover photo caused a stir. By dressing like Jesus, was Kanye supporting religion and showing his faith? Or was he mocking and rebelling against Christianity? The *Rolling Stone* cover upset many Christians, both among Kanye's fan base and in the general public. Some said that Kanye dressing up like Jesus made fun of their faith. The harshest critics said that Kanye was exploiting religious imagery simply to advance his career. Critics also blamed *Rolling Stone*, which had set up the photo shoot. Not surprisingly, Kanye himself shrugged off the criticism. By this time in his career, he was well accustomed to controversy.

Loop Dreams

As controversy stirred around him, Kanye continued with his work—both in the studio and outside of it. In 2006 the Kanye West Foundation launched its first project, Loop Dreams. The name was a play on *Hoop Dreams*, a 1994 documentary movie about two black teens who want professional basketball careers. Instead of basketball (hoops), Kanye wanted to encourage kids to make recording tracks (loops). When Kanye was young, he'd built his own music studio in his bedroom because he didn't have access to a studio at school or in his neighbor-hood. He figured he would have been a lot more interested in school if he had been able to study music there.

The Loop Dreams program began in a public middle school in Los Angeles. As part of the program, seventy-five eighth graders went to music classes every day. Using recording equipment provided by Loop Dreams, they learned to make loops and tracks. They also studied hip-hop culture, history, and trends and learned about career options in the music industry. The program was designed not only to interest kids in music but also to encourage them to stay in school.

Onstage and On Camera

In the fall of 2006, Kanye was nominated for MTV's European Music Awards in two categories: best hip-hop artist and best video for his song "Touch the Sky." At the televised awards show in November, held in Copenhagen, Denmark, Kanye won the best hip-hop artist award and made a gracious acceptance speech.

Later in the evening, the pre-senter announced the winner for best video. The English band Simian and the French duo Justice won for their collaboration "We Are Your Friends" (2006). In protest of his loss, Kanye walked onstage in front of the win-ners and grabbed the handheld

USA TODAY Snapshots®

If teens picked the Grammys

How "record of the year" nominees for Wednesday's Grammys fare with teen voters:

Boulevard of Broken Dreams
Green Day — 27%

Gold Digger
Kanye West — 17%

We Belong Together
Mariah Carey — 14%

Feel Good Inc.
Gorillaz featuring De La Soul — 10%

Hollaback Girl
Gwen Stefani — 9%

Source: Harris Interactive YouthQuery online survey of 1,092 teens ages 13–18, conducted Dec. 14–20.

By Tracey Wong Briggs and Julie Snider, USA TODAY, 2006

Speaking his mind: When Kanye lost out to Simian and Justice at the European Music Awards in 2006, he rushed the stage to protest.

microphone from the presenter. "Oh, hell no," he said. He then launched into a short tirade about how good his own video was and how expensive it had been to make. He cursed several times. "If I don't win, the award show loses credibility," he exclaimed. He then placed his arm around one of the winners and said, "It's nothing against you. I've never seen your video. It's nothing against you."

The winner responded, "You should have seen our video, man."

Later, MTV reporters asked Kanye if he had any further comment about not winning. He shrugged. "I just went up there and I talked my [mind] on stage," he told them. "Just as long as they don't edit my part, I'll be good."

The media had a field day criticizing Kanye for his onstage antics. Reporters called Kanye arrogant, rude, selfish, a sore loser, and more. They called his outburst a hissy fit and a tantrum. People were most critical about Kanye's outburst because he admitted that he'd never seen the winning video. He just assumed that he was the best—without even bothering to check out the competition.

IN FOCUS

Trouble for Evel Kanyevel

The 2006 video for Kanye's single "Touch the Sky" included a stunt where Kanye dresses up as a character named Evel Kanyevel. He wears a cape and a star-studded jumpsuit and pretends to fly over a canyon on a rocket. The video became a subject of controversy when famed stuntman Robert (Evel) Knievel sued Kanye for satirizing his name and image. Knievel was well known in the 1970s for his risky but impressive stunts, such as leaping over canyons on motorcycles. Knievel said that Kanye's video, which featured actress Pamela Anderson, was offensive and vulgar. Attorneys for the two men eventually settled the lawsuit but did not reveal the details of the settlement.

Kanye personally visited the elderly Knievel at his home in November 2007 to make amends. The two men got along well. "I thought he was a wonderful guy and quite a gentleman," Knievel remarked about Kanye. Knievel passed away a few days after the meeting.

Famous stunts: Evel Knievel attempted to rocket over the Snake River Canyon in Utah in 1974. Kanye's "Touch the Sky" video was based on Knievel's stunt.

August 22, 2005

Kanye West, Hip-Hop's Writer-in-Residence; Rapper/Producer Makes a Deeper Brand of Music

From the Pages of
USA TODAY

Kanye West's "Diamonds from Sierra Leone" addresses the horrors of the mining trade in the war-torn country, but when he first started writing the song, he wasn't thinking about precious stones.

"When I was saying 'Throw your diamonds in the sky' on the original, I was talking about the symbol fans throw up (thumb to thumb, index finger to index finger) at Roc-A-Fella concerts," he says of the song, which samples Shirley Bassey's James Bond theme "Diamonds Are Forever." "But God led me down this path. He put angels in my road to give me all this information. I didn't know I would wind up talking about blood diamonds."

West never embraced hip-hop's overriding thug motif. The Atlanta-born, Chicago-raised son of a college professor and a pastoral counselor doesn't have the 'hood credentials of most rap stars, and he never bothered trying to fake it. Even though he produced music for Jay-Z, Beanie Sigel and others, he had a hard time convincing record executives that he could rap as well. He never doubted it, but he knew his rhymes would be about something other than hustling on the streets.

"Don't I have the right to write about how things are affecting people?" he says. "But rap has always had this premise that if you didn't do it, you can't rap about it. I'm more of a writer or poet than a rapper. A rapper is all about image. Being a writer, I have the right to be a person."

That kind of thinking allows him to do such songs as "All Falls Down" (on debut *The College Dropout*), on which he confesses his love for expensive things while de crying materialism. On his new *Late Registration*, he again touches on a variety of atypical topics. "Crack Music" talks about the devastating effects of drugs in the black community. "Gold Digger," with Jamie Foxx, tells the tale of a guy who spent 18 years paying support for a child who turned out not to be his.

"I like to educate people," says West, who *Time* magazine this year named one of the 100 most influential people in the world. "I like to be the one that can reach people who don't like to pick up a book. I like to say something that might change someone's life."

The rapper says his father, Ray West, a former Black Panther and photojournalist, is helping him shape even stronger messages for two future albums, which will complete his "college series."

Ray West says he's not surprised that his son feels the need to teach.

"His mother (Donda West) and I never talked to him as if he was a kid," he says. "We always talked to him like he was an adult, and he sometimes had to catch up to the language. I'm a storyteller. . . . I've just sat back and been amazed at where he has taken it."

Kanye West has taken his unusual songs to lofty heights of radio airplay after being warned that a song like the Grammy-winning "Jesus Walks" would never get many spins. He also takes pains to maintain quality in everything he does. After nearly dying in an accident when he fell asleep at the wheel of his Lexus in October 2002, he decided that he'd never do shoddy work.

"When I had my accident, I was working on Beanie Sigel, Black Eyed Peas and Peedi Crakk, and let's just say that those tracks were not my best work," West says. "If I would have passed that night, that would have been the end of my legacy. Now when I go into the studio, I act like this could possibly be my last day."

He's just now getting used to celebrity. Though he used to boast to record executives that he would be bigger than Michael Jackson someday, he's not sure whether that's what he wants anymore.

"If anything, I'd sabotage my career to get some of my anonymity back, or to focus more on directing movies, which is another form of production," he says. "I would refuse to be as famous as Michael Jackson. Once I see it coming to that point, I would fall back, because I just want to be able to go to the movies [without being recognized]."

—Steve Jones

The Third Solo Album

In 2007 Kanye put together his third solo album, *Graduation*. Roc-A-Fella set the record's release date as September 11, 2007—the same day that rival rapper 50 Cent would release his album *Curtis*. Both new albums were highly anticipated in the rap and hip-hop world. Kanye wanted to best 50 Cent, so he challenged him to a contest to see whose album could sell more copies. No one expected Kanye to beat 50 Cent. In an interview, 50 Cent vowed to quit music if his album lost the contest.

Head-to-head: Kanye's *Graduation* outsold 50 Cent's *Curtis (right).* Here they play up their rivalry at the MTV Video Music Awards in 2007.

In the end, Kanye's album outsold 50 Cent's in a landslide. (But 50 Cent did not quit the music business as he had threatened.) Kanye's singles "Can't Tell Me Nothing" and "Stronger" became

Commencement: Kanye displays his *Graduation* CD during an autograph-signing session in Los Angeles in 2007.

hits. *Graduation* soon rose to the top of the charts, and Kanye received eight Grammy nominations for the album. Reviewers called the album quieter and more thoughtful than Kanye's two previous efforts.

USA TODAY Snapshots®

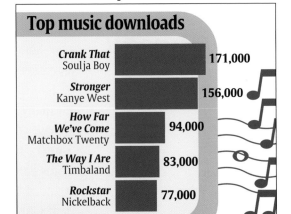

Top music downloads

Crank That Soulja Boy	**171,000**
Stronger Kanye West	**156,000**
How Far We've Come Matchbox Twenty	**94,000**
The Way I Are Timbaland	**83,000**
Rockstar Nickelback	**77,000**

Source: Nielsen SoundScan for week ending Sept. 9

By Ken Barnes and Veronica Salazar, USA TODAY, 2007

USA TODAY
A GANNETT COMPANY

CHAPTER SEVEN

Motherly love: Kanye and his mom were extremely close.

Heartbreak

Donda West lived in Los Angeles near Kanye. She helped manage his career and his foundation. Donda had struggled with her weight for many years and finally decided to have cosmetic surgery. Cosmetic surgery is not used to save a person's life or to treat a disease. Instead, it is meant to improve a person's appearance. In Donda's case, a surgeon was going to remove some fat from her stomach and her breasts.

Donda visited with a few surgeons in Los Angeles before choosing Jan Adams, who specialized in cosmetic surgery for women of color. Donda went in for the surgery on November 9, 2007. Before the operation, the medical staff administered an anesthetic, medication that made Donda unconscious.

Although the surgery went well, after the operation, the nurses had trouble waking Donda. This situation wasn't normal, and the staff was worried. Family members came to the medical center to drive Donda home, but she was still unconscious. In the recovery room, the family played Kanye's song "Hey Mama" next to Donda's ear. She roused at the sound of the music.

Dr. Adams sent Donda home, thinking she would recover normally. But he hadn't realized that she had a heart condition and that the surgery had further damaged her heart. Less than twenty-four hours after surgery, Donda died.

Kanye Reeling

Donda's family was heartbroken. They blamed Dr. Adams for not giving Donda a thorough medical exam before the surgery. California medical officials investigated the case. After the investigation, the state took away Dr. Adams's medical license. He also served a year in prison for his role in Donda's death.

Cosmetic surgeon: Jan Adams, the doctor who operated on Donda West, was held responsible for her death.

IN F⊕CUS

Good Out of Bad

The media spent a lot of time talking about Donda West's death. People asked whether Dr. Adams had acted improperly and whether, because of her heart condition, Donda should have been allowed to have surgery at all. Some people criticized Donda herself. They said she shouldn't have risked her life merely to change her appearance. Others blamed the doctor for not taking a complete medical history, which would have revealed the faults in her heart.

After her death, an examination revealed that Donda had died of heart disease and complications from the surgery. Dr. Adams was punished with a year in jail, and he also lost his medical license. The State of California also tightened its rules about cosmetic surgery, designed to prevent similar deaths in the future.

The loss of his mother hit Kanye especially hard. He had often referred to her as his best friend. By the time she passed away, she had also become a close business partner. She was the center of his support system, both personally and professionally. Her death devastated him.

But Kanye had a career to pursue. He did not allow himself to take time away from his business to grieve his mother's death. On some level, he believed his mother would have wanted it that way—for him to keep pushing forward and pursuing his dreams. So he moved through the world with a great ache in his heart.

At the 2008 Grammy Awards in February, Kanye performed his song "Hey Mama" as a tribute to his mother. He also performed his hit "Stronger." Kanye won in four categories that night: best rap solo performance for "Stronger," best rap duo performance for "Southside" with Common, best rap album for *Graduation*, and best rap song for "Good Life." But his personal loss made the victories bittersweet.

For Mama: *Top:* Kanye sings "Hey Mama," in honor of his mother, at the Grammy Awards in 2008. *Below left:* Kanye performs "Stronger" before the 2008 Grammy show. *Below right:* Kanye accepts one of his four awards that evening.

November 24, 2008

West Weighs What's Lost, Gained

<u>From the Pages of USA TODAY</u>

Having grown used to Kanye West luxuriating in the good life, the initial reaction to his brooding new opus [*808s and Heartbreak*] is surprise. After three albums chronicling the rags-to-riches rise of a college dropout, West now wants you to feel his pain.

A dark mood settles over his usually sunny outlook as West weighs what he has lost in recent months (his mother's unexpected death, a broken engagement) against the dubious value of what he has gained (fame and fortune). He knows that no amount of conspicuous consumption is going to ease his inner turmoil.

West deftly uses the 808 drum machine and Auto-Tune vocal effect to channel his feelings of hurt, anger and doubt through his well-crafted lyrics. And while some hip-hop fans may decry his decision to sing rather than rap (Lil Wayne and Young Jeezy provide what little rapping there is), he wisely brushes aside such creative limitations.

His career has been built on pushing boundaries and expanding possibilities. This time, [he] does it by stripping away the celebrity trappings and exposing his naked emotions.

—Steve Jones

Breakup: Kanye dated fashion designer Alexis Phifer for several years. They are seen here in 2008, shortly before they broke off their engagement.

A few months later, Kanye broke up with Alexis Phifer, his girlfriend of almost four years. Being suddenly separated from the two women closest to him left Kanye feeling depressed and isolated. He sometimes turned to alcohol to numb the pain.

Glow in the Dark

Kanye worked through his pain in the music studio. He began work on his fourth album during a period of moodiness and dark thoughts. Kanye had started a blog to keep in touch with his fans. On his blog in April 2008, he wrote, "The constant hours of creating helped me to keep from losing my mind in a bad way. [My video director] Chris Milk told me tragedy can produce great art and this is definitely true. I am a total mad man now, up till 3 A.M. every night, trying to fight pain, boredom and uncertainty with creativity. All that said, life is good."

That month, Kanye also began a world tour called Glow in the Dark.

Radiating: The Glow in the Dark Tour took Kanye all over the world. Here he performs in Wellington, New Zealand, in 2008.

He and guest artists Rihanna, Lupe Fiasco, Kid Cudi, N.E.R.D., Nas, and others performed at dozens of concert venues worldwide. The tour even included a special appearance by Jay-Z. The tour started off in North America, including major U.S. and Canadian cities. Then the performers toured through South America, Asia, and Europe.

Kanye, Fashion Icon

While his music career soared, another of Kanye's dreams began to come true. Kanye had always been interested in fashion. "I wanted to be a designer before I wanted to be a rapper," he said. Becoming a celebrity helped him make connections in the fashion world, since well-known designers often create costumes for music videos and dress rock stars in expensive outfits for big award shows. "Rapping has given me a plateau to meet with some really dope [excellent] designers," Kanye said.

Red-hot sneaks: Kanye shows one of his Louis Vuitton sneakers to fashion designer Marc Jacobs during Paris Fashion Week in 2009.

IN FOCUS

The Louis Vuitton Don

Kanye's fondness for fashion, especially for expensive brands such as Louis Vuitton, earned him the nickname the Louis Vuitton Don. *Don* is another word for a nobleman or an important person.

Kanye looked forward to the day when he could have his own clothing line. Many celebrities have professional designers create their fashion lines, but Kanye wanted to do the designing himself.

In early 2008, Kanye designed a collection of men's sneakers for Louis Vuitton, a well-known luxury brand, most famous for its shoulder bags, suitcases, and other leather goods. Louis Vuitton even hosted Kanye's thirtieth birthday party at its main store in New York City. The guest list included many hip-hop stars. During the celebration, Louis Vuitton publicly announced Kanye's upcoming shoe line.

In Your Face

By 2008 Kanye West was a major star. His picture appeared in celebrity magazines and on show business websites. Tens of thousands of people wanted to know what Kanye was up to, whom he was dating, and where he would be performing. A photographer could make thousands of dollars by selling just one picture of Kanye to a tabloid newspaper or website. Photographers often followed Kanye in his car and on the streets, and he didn't like it.

In early September 2008, Kanye and his road manager, Don Crowley, went to the Los Angeles International Airport to catch a flight to Hawaii. Near the ticketing counter, photographers for some tabloid newspapers tried to take Kanye's picture. Kanye asked the

Tabloids: Kanye doesn't like being hounded by photographers. Here, he yells at a videographer in 2009.

photographers to back off, but they kept hounding him.

Angry, Kanye and Crowley tussled with the photographers. During the fight, Kanye grabbed an expensive camera from a photographer and threw it to the ground, smashing it. Crowley then smashed another photographer's camera. Local police arrested Kanye and Crowley for their violent behavior.

A judge dropped the most serious charges against Kanye, but he still had to pay for the broken equipment, take anger management classes, and perform community service as punishment for his misdeeds. Kanye fulfilled the community service requirement by doing fifty hours of work for the Red Cross, an international health, safety, and rescue organization. The incident with the photographers further added to Kanye's reputation as a hothead.

June 10, 2009

West Drops in to Talk about Education

<u>From the Pages of</u>
<u>USA TODAY</u>

Kanye West has a humble side, and he's not afraid to show it. "I'm a very, very down-to-earth person," the rapper says in a phone interview, downplaying much-talked-about award show tantrums. "I mean, I'm just a very honest person with music and with supporters and at award shows. It's like I'm at war or like I'm on the court. But in real life, I'm laid-back and just want everyone to have a good time and help as many people as possible."

On Thursday he'll do just that by headlining the Kanye West Benefit Concert at the Chicago Theatre. The event will benefit the Kanye West Foundation, a charity designed to help kids stay in school. The foundation was created by West's mother, Donda, who died in 2007 after complications following plastic surgery. "It just makes me happy that we have really great people involved that can help to keep my mother's vision of education in an innovative way alive," West says.

West is passionate about the foundation because it also promotes a music production program designed to motivate students to stay in school and graduate. It's the very thing that West, who famously titled his debut album *The College Dropout*, wishes he'd had. He jokes that maybe he would have stayed in school longer. (He dropped out of Chicago State University, where his mother was the English department chair.)

"I thought back to when I was in high school: I was very into music, but the equipment was really expensive and hard to get a hold of. The basketball court at school was free. Or it was free to play a violin or a drum set, but the way music on the radio is made, there was nothing in high school that helped with that," he says. So far the West Foundation has helped 200 kids in Los Angeles learn to write music and use music studio equipment, and West hopes in the future he's able to expand his efforts.

And as for his hip-hop persona? "When I go back to rapping," he says of the fifth studio album he's working on, "I might have to go back to war. I just might have to."

—Kelley L. Carter

Soulful: Kanye performs at the 2009 Grammy Awards. His jacket features the red broken heart pin that he wore in the promotional pictures for his *808s and Heartbreak* album.

A New Album

In November 2008, Kanye released his fourth solo album, *808s and Heartbreak*. Many of the songs on the album reflected Kanye's sadness at the death of his mother and the breakup with Alexis. Many were soulful ballads instead of Kanye's usual upbeat raps. The rapping on the album was primarily done by guest artists.

Kanye has a good singing voice—but it's not perfect. To improve his voice, Kanye sang most of the tracks on the record using a computer program called Auto-Tune. The program makes minor adjustments to a singer's voice. If he or she sings off-key, Auto-Tune corrects the mistake. Kanye also used the program to give his voice an icy, robotic sound, perhaps to reveal his wounded state of mind. Kanye also used a Roland TR-808 drum machine to give the album its booming beats. The 808 of the album title refers to this machine.

IN FOCUS

Auto-Tune

A lot of professional singers use Auto-Tune to make their voices sound better. Its use is a bit controversial, however. Supporters of the software like it because it can make a mediocre singer sound like a good singer and can make a good singer sound like a great singer. But some critics say that records made with Auto-Tune aren't authentic. They give a false impression of what a singer really sounds like. Many note that even the best singers aren't always perfect and that the software takes away the small quirks that make each person's voice interesting and unique.

Stealing the Mike, Again

Coming into the 2009 Video Music Awards in September, Kanye had a clear favorite. He had fallen in love with the song and video for "Single Ladies (Put a Ring on It)" by Beyoncé. On the red carpet, he told reporters that Beyoncé's video was one of the best he'd ever seen. He also said it was exciting to have artists compete for the top prizes at award shows. "I think it's fun to have a friendly competition of people pushing to be the best artist in the world," he said.

Kanye fully expected Beyoncé's video to win in the category of best female video. Instead, the award went to pop and country singer Taylor Swift for her song "You Belong with Me" (2008). Watching Swift win the award, Kanye became furious on Beyoncé's behalf.

Taylor Swift came up onstage and took the handheld microphone to begin her acceptance speech. She said how excited she was, how much she had dreamed of winning such an award, and how little she had expected it to ever really happen.

In the middle of her remarks, Kanye burst onto the stage. He ripped the microphone from Taylor's hand and spoke into it. "Yo Taylor, I'm

Jumping in uninvited: Kanye jumps onstage as Taylor Swift accepts her award during the 2009 MTV Video Music Awards.

really happy for you," he said. "I'll let you finish." Then he turned and pointed into the audience, where Beyoncé was sitting. "But Beyoncé has one of the best videos of all time." Then he shrugged, handed the microphone back to Taylor, and walked offstage.

The crowd booed Kanye for his rudeness. Camera footage showed Beyoncé's wide-eyed face in the crowd. She appeared to be somewhat flattered by Kanye's compliment but equally shocked and horrified by Kanye stealing Taylor's moment.

Stunned and unsure what else to do, Taylor Swift exited the stage. Later in the show, Beyoncé won an award in another category, best video of the year. When Beyoncé came onstage to accept her award, she invited Taylor Swift up to properly finish her acceptance speech. Everyone applauded the gesture.

Backlash

The next day, media outlets ran stark headlines about Kanye's stunt. Once again, reporters called him arrogant, rude, self-important, prone to tantrums, and attention seeking. People who did not follow hip-hop before suddenly became aware of Kanye—in a highly negative light. Kanye found himself under intense pressure—personally, professionally, and publicly.

Coming back: Kanye makes an appearance during a Jay-Z concert at New York's Yankee Stadium in 2010.

Runaway

■■■■

Kanye's interruption of Taylor Swift marked the last stage of a long emotional decline. The media refused to let the incident go. And Kanye began to realize how far away he was from the person he wanted to be. He knew he needed to apologize.

Kanye apologized to Taylor on his blog and via Twitter almost immediately after the incident. Next, he apologized publicly on *The Tonight Show*

Regret: Taylor Swift leaves *The View* after receiving an apology from Kanye over the phone.

with Jay Leno. But he knew a personal apology was in order too. About a week after the VMA broadcast, Taylor appeared as a guest on ABC's morning talk show *The View*. Kanye called in and surprised her with an on-air apology, which she accepted.

A Break from the Limelight

Despite the apologies, the media stayed on Kanye's case. Amid the frenzy, friends advised Kanye to get out of the limelight for a while. Kanye knew they were right. He needed some time and space to deal with himself and his grief.

So Kanye left the United States and left music behind for a while too. He traveled to Japan and stayed there for several months. He wanted to lie low, away from the media, and try to get his head together. Next, he moved to Rome, Italy, where he turned his attention to fashion design. He interned at Fendi, an Italian clothing company, to learn more about the fashion industry. He shadowed the Fendi designers to see how they worked. He also gave the designers his own design ideas so he could learn from their feedback.

Of his self-imposed exile, Kanye remarked, "It was some real . . . rock-star-banished-from-America, come-pull-your-life-together stuff." He called the Taylor Swift incident a wake-up call, alerting him that he was spinning out of control. He blamed alcohol in part for his behavior.

Back in the United States

Eventually, Kanye felt ready to work on music again. He traveled to Oahu, Hawaii, where he began work on his fifth solo album, *My Beautiful Dark Twisted Fantasy*. Kid Cudi, Alicia Keys, and Rihanna contributed to the album as guest artists.

When he returned home to Los Angeles, Kanye appeared on *The Ellen DeGeneres Show* and spoke about his departure from the spotlight. He explained that he had needed time away to regain a perspective on his life, his music, and his fame. "It was the first time I'd [taken a break] since my mom died," he told Ellen. "It was the first time I'd stopped since I actually made it [became a star]."

On the talk show, Kanye also discussed his behavior toward Taylor Swift. But while he acknowledged his own rudeness, he did not apologize for the underlying motivation for his actions. He explained to Ellen that

Back at work: In Oahu, Hawaii, in 2009, Kanye begins work on his fifth solo album.

IN F⊕CUS

Million-Dollar Smile

During Kanye's October 2010 appearance on *The Ellen DeGeneres Show*, after the two talked about Taylor Swift and Donda's death, Ellen brought up a lighter subject. She pointed to Kanye's teeth and asked, "What's with the grille [mouth] here?"

Kanye flashed a winning smile. The camera came in for a close-up and revealed a row of jewels sparkling in Kanye's mouth. Kanye explained that he had replaced several of his bottom teeth with gold and diamonds.

Ellen was flabbergasted. She wanted to know why Kanye had changed his real teeth for gold and diamonds. "I mean, there's just certain stuff that rock stars are supposed to do," Kanye told Ellen. The audience laughed and cheered.

Bling: Kanye shows off his gold and diamond teeth on *The Ellen DeGeneres Show*.

African American artists had been denied honors "for years and years and years and years." He suggested that Swift had been favored for the award because she is white. Beyoncé is black. By speaking up for Beyoncé, he felt he was standing up for racial equality.

The Fifth Album

Kanye released *My Beautiful Dark Twisted Fantasy* in 2010. The record featured the hit singles "Power" and "Runaway."

November 22, 2010

Kanye's "Fantasy" Contains a Beautiful Reality

<u>From the Pages of</u>
<u>USA TODAY</u>

Kanye West is arguably popular music's most compelling and controversial figure. In the past six years, he's been acclaimed for four groundbreaking albums and disdained for his public fits of pique and rampant narcissism. The audacious new *My Beautiful Dark Twisted Fantasy* (**** out of four) opens a window into an ego that is often tripping, thus exposing the insecurities and foibles that fuel West's boundless creativity and grandiose ambitions.

West threw himself into his music during a self-imposed exile from the spotlight after his embarrassing Taylor Swift moment at MTV's 2009 Video Music Awards. He stayed in the studio, working through personal issues and pouring those feelings into songs. Though he's rooted in a genre where rappers shield their emotions, West succeeds by doing the opposite. The result is an epic, adventurous aural mélange [mix] that easily outstrips anything he's done.

"I just needed time alone, with my thoughts," he says on "Power." "Got treasures in my mind but couldn't open up my own vault."

He not only gets the treasures out, he shapes them into sonic jewels that sparkle with contributions from pop's and hip-hop's glitterati [stars]. The anthemic "All of the Lights" alone features a dozen stars, including Rihanna, Alicia Keys, The-Dream, Kid Cudi, Fergie and Elton John.

With the help of such producers as The RZA, Bink!, No I.D., Mike Dean and Jeff Bhasker, West unleashes an array of sonic flavors—old school hip-hop, progressive rock, R&B, classical music—and deftly mixes and matches them.

On the wrenching "Runaway" (basis for a 30-minute West-directed short film released in October), he confesses to his problems sustaining relationships: "Never

Movie time: Kanye attends the New York premiere of his short film *Runaway* in 2010.

was much of a romantic/I could never take the intimacy/And I know it did damage/ Cus the look in your eyes is killin' me."

Still, he's hardly throwing a self-pity party. On the escalating ego arms race that is "Monster"—with Jay-Z, Rick Ross, Nicki Minaj and Bon Iver—West declares, "My presence is a present." His piece de resistance [highlight], though, is "Blame Game," a brooding, nearly eight-minute tale of a couple with irreconcilable differences that plays out with growing hostility over John Legend's moody piano work.

With the success he's had, West could settle into a predictable hitmaking rut. Instead, the only thing predictable about him is his unremitting drive to make his next project better than his last.

—Steve Jones

Surprise show: Kanye performs with Justin Vernon of the band Bon Iver at the Bowery Ballroom in New York City in 2010.

Kanye also created a thirty-five-minute short film (also called *Runaway*) based on the album. Released on DVD, the film featured nine songs from the album (instead of just one for the typical music video). "I've always had this dream of having a full length [film] that showed visuals for all these songs that deserve videos. . . . A DVD you can pop in [instead of] YouTubeing it over and over," Kanye explained.

The *Runaway* video tells the story of a phoenix, a mythical bird.

"As his career progressed throughout the early 21st century, West shattered certain stereotypes about rappers, becoming a superstar on his own terms without adapting his appearance, his rhetoric [way of talking], or his music to fit any one musical mold."

—*Billboard* magazine website, n.d.

She comes to Earth and faces discrimination from human beings. The message of the film is about how people respond to those who are different.

Watch the Throne

In November 2010, Kanye and Jay-Z began work on a collaborative album called *Watch the Throne*, with guest artists Beyoncé, Mr Hudson, Frank Ocean, and others. The artists recorded various tracks in cities around the world, including Sydney, Australia; London, England; and Paris, France. The album incorporated a deep range of background music, including orchestral and rock samples.

The lyrics continued Kanye's trend of mixing pop influences with heavier political reflections and social commentary. Songs such as "Made in America" make references to civil rights, including Kanye's own family history of protest. "Murder to Excellence" deals with crime in black communities and the limited job opportunities for black Americans. The album's overarching

Together again: Kanye and Jay-Z celebrate the release of their *Watch the Throne* album.

message is about the relationship of black men such as Kanye and Jay-Z to wealth, celebrity, and power. For instance, the song "New Day" speaks to their future sons about fame." On "Niggas in Paris," the two address their journeys from being unknown, struggling musicians to being recognized the world over.

Number one on the *Billboard* charts: The *Watch the Throne* CD has a glittery cover. It was released in August 2011.

When it debuted in August 2011, *Watch the Throne* hit number one on the *Billboard* chart immediately. It sold 436,000 copies in the first week. The album received widely positive reviews. By the end of 2011, it had sold more than 1.1 million copies in the United States alone.

"I try to make music that touches people because I feel like I am the people. I'm a part of them."

—Kanye West, 2010

Occupy Wall Street

One of the biggest news events of late 2011 was the Occupy Wall Street movement. The movement brought people together to protest financial injustices in the United States, such as the fact that only 1 percent of Americans take home nearly 25 percent of the nation's income and control about 40 percent of the nation's wealth. Occupy Wall Street protesters declared themselves representatives of the other 99 percent of citizens. They demanded financial equality for all Americans.

In mid-September, the protesters set up camp in Zuccotti Park near Wall Street—the center of New York City's financial district. The movement quickly spread. Protesters set up camps in parks in many cities across the United States and around the world.

In New York, many celebrities stopped by the encampment to show support for the protests. One fall afternoon, Kanye and fellow hip-hop mogul Russell Simmons visited the camp. Kanye was wearing gold chains around his neck. He flashed the crowd a glimpse of his diamond teeth.

Joining the protesters: Kanye visits Occupy Wall Street in New York in October 2011.

IN F◐CUS

His Own Line

In 2010 Kanye finally created his own fashion line, DW by Kanye West, a clothing line for women. The initials DW stand for Donda West. Kanye developed the line in collaboration with designers from the French fashion house Givenchy.

Every year, the fashion industry holds a series of shows in fashion capitals such as New York, London, Paris, and Milan (Italy). The shows go on for a week at a time. They feature the latest collections from established and up-and-coming fashion designers.

In October 2011, Kanye showed a collection at Paris Fashion Week. Many of his famous fashion designer friends, including actors-turned-designers Mary-Kate and Ashley Olsen, were in attendance. The fashion press also came to see what Kanye had designed. Kanye showed again at Paris Fashion Week in March 2012. The collections featured a lot of leather pants and jackets, fur coats, and slinky dresses.

Reactions to his clothing were mixed. Many fashion reporters said his designs lacked vision. Others were even more critical. They said Kanye's clothing was unflattering and fit poorly on the runway models. In turn, Kanye had some blunt words for the press. "If they don't understand it [my clothing], they don't understand it," he told a reporter. Then he ended the interview.

On the catwalk: Models wearing Kanye's designs strut the runway in Paris in 2011.

Kanye did not make any press statements about what he was doing at the camp. But some people felt he was not really there to show support for the protesters at all. By displaying his expensive jewelry, he seemed to be identifying with the wealthy 1 percent much more than the financially struggling 99 percent of Americans.

Around the same time, Jay-Z began producing and selling T-shirts and other merchandise that said "Occupy All Streets." However, profits from the sale of the shirts did not go toward aid for the protesters. Occupy Wall Street members were upset with Jay-Z for trading on their movement's name to make money—especially since Jay-Z has plenty of money of his own.

Kanye Imagines His Impact

During the Watch the Throne Tour with Jay-Z, Kanye spoke to reporters about how he wants to be remembered when he dies. He imagined world leaders attending his funeral, grateful for the impact he had made on them. Although not naming anyone specifically, he said he envisioned important people saying things like, "Kanye gave me my shot here. He told me to believe in myself." Kanye admitted, "I want to affect people like that."

Kanye has never stopped believing in himself and in the gifts he has to offer the world creatively. "Okay, I'm doing music, but there's a bigger plan for me," Kanye said. "I wasn't given this power for no reason. And now it's starting to open up."

The single-minded passion that developed in Kanye as a child has not waned. Kanye wants to be the best, nothing less. He knows that he has to work hard every day to keep himself on the cutting edge of the music industry. "It's a pursuit, and it's a responsibility," he says. "If people have done things before, you should be able to surpass them. I'm on a pursuit of awesomeness. Excellence is the bare minimum."

Kanye knows he is just one person, doing one person's work. He knows he is not alone in the struggle for awesomeness and impact, the struggle to make the world a better place.

August 5, 2011

Jay-Z and Kanye West's "Throne" Could Bear Watching

<u>From the Pages of</u>
<u>USA TODAY</u>

Jay-Z and Kanye West ignite interest whenever either of them releases a new album, but they're turning Monday's digital debut of *Watch the Throne*, their first full-album collaboration, into a cultural event.

Between them, they have a slew of chart-topping, critically acclaimed platinum albums (Jay-Z's 11 studio albums have sold 28 million-plus copies, West's five have sold more than 11 million), and they've been working together for more than a decade. But this long-anticipated project between mentor Jay-Z, 41, and protégé West, 34, finds them on equal footing, and hip-hop observers who've heard the album say they've pushed each other to new creative heights.

They've kept the music tightly under wraps, playing the album for small groups of tastemakers and journalists who have described the project as having plenty of the two rappers' characteristic swagger, but also a degree of social consciousness and introspection. *Throne* arrives exclusively on iTunes, then hits stores and additional digital outlets on August 12.

Tickets for the companion Watch the Throne Tour also go on sale Monday at Ticketmaster and Live Nation. The 23-date tour launches October 29 in Atlanta and wraps up December 18 in Vancouver, British Columbia.

The music is a step forward for both artists, says Jermaine Hall, *Vibe* editor in chief. West handled much of the production with help from RZA, The Neptunes, Q-Tip, Swizz Beatz, and others. Beyoncé, Frank Ocean and Mr Hudson are the only guest vocalists.

"Sonically, it's really an amazing record," Hall says. "The lyrics are extra-sharp, and while there's a little materialism that some people might not be into, what can't be questioned is the quality of the lines."

The superstars share mutual respect, but there's a competitive edge to their work, says Chuck Creekmur, co-founder/CEO of Allhiphop.com. "Jay-Z recently called Kanye an artistic genius, and Kanye calls Jay his big brother," Creekmur says.

"Kanye has worked hard to get where he's mentioned in the same sentence as Jay-Z. "My hope is this album causes other artists to push the envelope. This is one of those albums that really brings back that new-car smell to hip-hop."

—Steve Jones

Standing proud: Kanye performs at the 2011 Essence Music Festival at the Superdome in New Orleans. Kanye hopes to push rap and hip-hop forward.

"I'm not trying to say that what I'm doing is the most important thing that's happening on the planet," he insists. "But what I'm saying is, what I'm doing is necessary. Just like if there's one teacher teaching in a class. What she's doing is necessary."

Deep down, what Kanye wants most is for the next musical generation to carry on his legacy. He doesn't want his musical impact to end with him. He is trying to inspire a movement. He is trying to push rap and hip-hop forward and to push society toward greater social consciousness—a task that is much bigger than one person. He says, "I wanna know that when I'm gone, there'll be ten people that will go up and grab that mike."

TIMELINE

1977: Kanye Omari West is born in Atlanta, Georgia.

1980: Donda and Ray West divorce. Donda and Kanye move to Chicago, Illinois.

1987: Donda and Kanye move to China, where Donda teaches at Nanjing University for a year.

1995: Kanye graduates from Polaris High School in Chicago. Kanye attends the American Academy of Art for one semester.

1996: Kanye enrolls in and drops out of Chicago State University.

2000: Kanye creates some beats for rapper Jay-Z.

2001: Kanye moves to Newark, New Jersey. Kanye produces Jay-Z's album *The Blueprint.*

2002: Kanye raps as a guest artist on Jay-Z's album *The Blueprint 2.* Roc-A-Fella Records gives Kanye a record deal. Kanye breaks his jaw in a car accident in Los Angeles after falling asleep at the wheel.

2003: Kanye's "Through the Wire" is released as a single. Kanye and Donda West establish the Kanye West Foundation.

2004: Kanye's first album, *The College Dropout,* debuts. Kanye tours the United States as the opening act for Usher's Truth Tour. Kanye walks out of the American Music Awards after losing the best new artist award to Gretchen Wilson.

2005: Kanye wins two Grammy Awards. During the MTV Special "All Eyes on Kanye West," Kanye speaks out against homophobia (discrimination against gay people) in hip-hop. Kanye's album *Late Registration* debuts. At a live Hurricane Katrina fund-raiser, Kanye blurts "George Bush doesn't care about black people."

2006: Kanye poses as Jesus for the cover of *Rolling Stone* magazine. The Kanye West Foundation launches its Loop Dreams project. Kanye rushes the stage and makes a tirade when he doesn't win for best video at the MTV European Music Awards. Robert (Evel) Knievel sues Kanye for satirizing his name and image in a music video.

2007: Kanye's album *Graduation* debuts on the same day 50 Cent's album *Curtis* debuts. Donda West dies from complications after cosmetic surgery.

2008: Kanye wins four Grammy Awards. Kanye and Alexis Phifer break off their engagement. Kanye performs with other artists at the Glow in the Dark Tour. Kanye designs a collection of men's sneakers for the Louis Vuitton label. Kanye and his road manager fight with photographers at the Los Angeles Airport. Kanye releases his album *808s and Heartbreak*.

2009: Kanye takes the mike from Taylor Swift at the MTV Video Music Awards and declares that Beyoncé should have won for best video instead of Taylor. Kanye takes time away from the spotlight and travels to Japan, Italy, and Hawaii.

2010: Kanye's album *My Beautiful Dark Twisted Fantasy* debuts. Kanye creates a line of women's clothing called DW Kanye West.

2011: Kanye and Jay-Z's album *Watch the Throne* debuts. Kanye and Jay-Z's Watch the Throne Tour circles

Presidential hip-hop: Kanye West performs at the Youth Ball after the inauguration of President Barack Obama in January 2009.

North America. Kanye and Russell Simmons visit Occupy Wall Street.

2012: Kanye debuts his fall 2012 clothing line at Paris Fashion Week.

GLOSSARY

break: in hip-hop music, the brief part in a song during which the band drops out and the rhythm section takes over

disc jockey (DJ): a musician who uses record albums and a turntable to create new sounds

emcee: another name for a rapper. The term comes from MC, which stands for master of ceremonies.

freestyling: in rap, improvising or making up a rap on the spot while performing

gangsta rap: a form of hip-hop that focuses on gang life. Gansta rap originated in California during the late 1980s.

hip-hop: a type of popular music that often features rapping along with background music created by a DJ

producer: the person who oversees the planning and financing of a television show, a movie, or a play or who oversees the recording of a song or an album

scratching: the technique of moving a playing record back and forth rhythmically beneath the record-player needle

SOURCE NOTES

6 Larry Copeland, "Kanye and Jay-Z Bring Rap Royalty to Atlanta," *USA TODAY*, October 31, 2011, D2.

9 Donda West, *Raising Kanye*, with Karen Hunter (New York: Simon and Schuster, 2007), Kindle edition, 172–174.

10 Ibid., 205–206.

12 Donda West, *Raising Kanye: Life Lessons from the Mother of a Hip-Hop Superstar*, with Karen Hunter (New York: Simon and Schuster, 2007), print edition, 54.

21 Advameg, "Kanye West: Biography," *Encyclopedia of World Biography*, n.d., http://www.notablebiographies.com/news/Sh-Z/West-Kanye .html (March 19, 2012).

23 *Billboard*, "Kanye West: Biography," n.d., http://www.billboard .com/artist/kanye-west/bio/322005#/artist/kanye-west/bio/322005 (March 19, 2012).

24 West, *Raising Kanye*, print, 113.

29 Josh Tyrangiel, "Why You Can't Ignore Kanye," *Time*, August 21, 2005, http://www.time.com/time/magazine/article/0,9171,1096499,00 .html (March 19, 2012).

33 Advameg, "Kanye West," *Encyclopedia of World Biography*, n.d., http://www.notablebiographies.com/newsmakers2/2006-Ra-Z/ West-Kanye.html (March 19, 2012).

36 Advameg, "Kanye West: Biography."

36 Cengage Learning, "Black History Month: Kanye West," *Gale*, n.d., http://www.gale.cengage.com/free_resources/bhm/bio/west_k.htm (March 12, 2012).

36 West, *Raising Kanye*, print, 135.

39 West, *Raising Kanye*, Kindle, 1,882–1,884.

44–45 James Montgomery. "Heard Him Say! A Timeline of Kanye West's Public Outbursts," *MTV News*, September 12, 2007, http://www.mtv .com/news/articles/1569536/kanye-wests-public-outbursts-timeline.jhtml (March 12, 2012).

45 West, *Raising Kanye*, Kindle, 2,242–2,243.

46–47 Montgomery, "Heard Him Say!"

53 Advameg, "Kanye West."

53 Rob Sheffield, "Review: Kanye West, Late Registration, Def Jam," *Rolling Stone*, August 25, 2005, http://www.rollingstone.com/music

/albumreviews/late-registration-20050825 (March 19, 2012).

56 Montgomery, "Heard Him Say!"

56 West, *Raising Kanye*, Kindle, 849–850.

59 West, *Raising Kanye*, print, 185.

62 Bill Chappell, "Bush Says Kanye West's Attack Was Low Point of His Presidency; West Agrees," *NPR.org*, November 3, 2010, http:// www.npr.org/blogs/thetwo-way/2010/11/03/131052717/bush-says-kanye-west-s-attack-was-low-point-of-his-presidency (April 21, 2012).

63 "Kanye West Responds to George Bush on the Today Show," *YouTube* video, 7:28, from an interview by Matt Lauer televised by NBC in November 2010, posted by "MBDTF," November 11, 2010, http:// www.youtube.com/watch?v=4ZVYZkD1tMk&feature=related (March 19, 2012).

66 MTV, "Kanye West Crashing Stage at EMA's after Losing to Justice," from the MTV European Music Awards, YouTube video, 2:07, posted by "maxxtothemaxx2," October 12, 2007, http://www.youtube.com /watch?v=QTJxj7a9-DA (March 19, 2012).

66 Ibid.

67 *USA Today*, "Evel Knievel, Kanye West Settle Lawsuit," November 27, 2007, http://www.usatoday.com/life/music/news/2007-11-27-kanye-knievel_N.htm (April 16, 2012).

77 Jon Bream, "Kanye West: Is He Rap's Greatest Rock Star or Just Lost in Space?, *Minneapolis Star Tribune*, June 10, 2008, http://www .popmatters.com/pm/article/kanye-west-is-he-raps-greatest-rock-star-or-just-lost-in-space (March 19, 2012).

78 Robert C. Schaller Jr., *Kanye West: A Biography* (Santa Barbara, CA: Greenwood, 2008), Kindle edition, 471–473.

83 *Access Hollywood*, "Why Did Kanye West Take a Year Off?" *Internet Movie Database*, October 2010, http://www.imdb.com/video/hulu /vi2416417049/ (March 19, 2012).

84 Daniel Kreps, "Kanye West Storms the VMAs Stage during Taylor Swift's Speech," *Rolling Stone*, September 13, 2009, http://www .rollingstone.com/music/news/kanye-west-storms-the-vmas-stage-during-taylor-swifts-speech-20090913 (April 21, 2012).

87 "Kanye on Ellen Full Interview," YouTube video, 10:58, posted by "bigboindabrook," October 19, 2010, from the *Ellen DeGeneres Show*

televised on October 19, 2010, http://www.youtube.com
/watch?v=PSCcD9Djj5M (March 19, 2012).

88 Ibid.

88 Ibid.

89 "Kanye on Ellen Full Interview," YouTube video.

92 Simon Vozick-Levinson, "Kanye West's Busy News Week," *Music Mix*,
October 20, 2010, http://music-mix.ew.com/2010/10/20/
kanye-west-suicide-teeth-news/ (March 19, 2012).

92 *Billboard*, "Kanye West: Biography."

94 *Access Hollywood*, "Why Did Kanye West Take a Year Off?."

96 Eric Wilson, "Kanye West Lets the Clothes Talk for Him," *New York
Times*, March 6, 2012, http://runway.blogs.nytimes.com/2012/03/06/
kanye-west-lets-the-clothes-talk-for-him/ (March 7, 2012).

97 NME, "Kanye West: 'I Want the Leaders of the World to Attend My
Funeral When I Die'—Video" *NME*, December 3, 2011, http://www
.nme.com/news/kanye-west/60764 (March 19, 2012).

97 Ibid.

97 Ibid.

99 Ibid.

99 Ibid.

SELECTED BIBLIOGRAPHY

Billboard. "Artist Bio: Kanye West." N.d. http://www.billboard.com/artist
/kanye-west/322005#/artist/kanye-west/bio/322005 (March 19, 2012).

Bream, Jon. "Kanye West: Is He Rap's Greatest Rock Star or Just Lost in
Space?" *Minneapolis Star Tribune,* June 10, 2008. http://www
.popmatters.com/pm/article/kanye-west-is-he-raps-greatest-rock-star-
or-just-lost-in-space (March 19, 2012).

Shakur, Tupac. *The Rose That Grew from Concrete.* New York: MTV Books,
2009.

WatchMojo.com. "Touch the Sound: A Sound Journey with Evelyn Glennie
(The Life and Career of Kanye West)." *Internet Movie Database.* N.d.
http://www.imdb.com/video/hulu/vi816879641/ (March 19, 2012).

West, Donda. *Raising Kanye: Life Lessons from the Mother of a Hip-Hop
Superstar.* With Karen Hunter. New York: Simon and Schuster, 2007.

West, Kanye. *Glow in the Dark.* New York: Rizzoli, 2009.

——. *Through the Wire: Lyrics and Illumination.* Illustrations by Bill Plympton.
New York: Atria, 2008.

FURTHER READING

Golus, Carrie. *Russell Simmons.* Minneapolis: Twenty-First Century Books,
2012.

——. *Tupac Shakur.* Minneapolis: Twenty-First Century Books, 2010.

Heos, Bridget. *Jay-Z.* New York: Rosen Classroom, 2009.

La Bella, Laura. *Kanye West.* New York: Rosen Publishing Group, 2009.

Sacks, Nathan. *American Hip-Hop: Rappers, DJs, and Hard Beats.* Minneapolis:
Twenty-First Century Books, 2013.

Waters, Rosa. *Beyoncé.* Broomall, PA: Mason Crest Publishers, 2007.

——. *Hip Hop: A Short History.* Broomall, PA: Mason Crest Publishers, 2007.

Weicker, Gretchen. *Kanye West: Hip Hop Star.* Berkeley Heights, NJ: Enslow
Publishers, 2009.

DISCOGRAPHY

Solo Studio Albums

The College Dropout. New York: Roc-A-Fella Records, 2004.

Late Registration. New York: Roc-A-Fella Records/Def Jam Recordings, 2005.

Graduation. New York: Roc-A-Fella Records/Mercury, 2007.

808s and Heartbreak. New York: Roc-A-Fella Records, 2008.

My Beautiful Dark Twisted Fantasy. New York: Roc-A Fella Records, 2010.

Creative Collaborations

Watch the Throne, with Jay-Z. New York: Roc-A-Fella Records/Def Jam
    Recordings/RocNation, 2011.

Duo: Kanye collaborates with singer Rihanna at the NBA All-Star Game halftime
show in 2011.

WEBSITES

Hip-Hop: Beyond Beats and Rhymes
http://www.pbs.org/independentlens/hiphop/index.htm
This website, a companion to a film of the same name, explores underlying issues in hip-hop culture, including violence and racial identify. The website includes a timeline of hip-hop history and a glossary of terms.

Hip-Hop/Urban
http://allmusic.com/explore/metastyle/hip-hop-urban-d4483
This website introduces hip-hop music and its various subgenres, such as old-school rap and pop-rap. Visitors can click on links to specific subgenres, artists, and songs to learn more.

Kanye West
http://allmusic.com/artist/kanye-west-p353484
This site from allmusic.com includes a biography of Kanye West, a discography, a song index, and more.

Kanye West
http://www.billboard.com/artist/kanye-west/322005#/artist/kanye-west/bio/322005
This website from *Billboard* magazine offers a biography of Kanye West, along with discussions of his work and his status in the music industry.

Roc-A-Fella
http://www.islanddefjam.com/default.aspx?labelID=75
Visitors to this website can learn about the latest releases and goings-on at Roc-A-Fella Records, Kanye's record label.

"Through the Wire," 35, 36, 38
Tonight Show, The, 86
"Touch the Sky," 52, 65, 67
Twista, 38, 42

Usher, 41, 43

Vanderpoel Elementary School, 9
Video Music Awards, 83–84, 87, 90
View, The, 87

Watch the Throne, 93–94, 98
Watch the Throne Tour, 4–6, 97, 98
"We Major," 51
West, Donda, 7–8, 9, 10–12, 18, 19,
    20, 21, 23, 24, 33–34, 36, 38–39,
    45, 56, 69, 72–73, 74, 76, 81, 89;
    death of, 73
West, Kanye Omari: arrested, 80;
    awards, 46–47, 50, 58, 65–66,
    69, 74; birth of, 7; blog, 77, 86;
    childhood, 8–9, 10–13, 15–17,
    28; at college, 18–19; criticism
    of, 39, 40, 63, 64, 66, 84–85,
    97; diamond teeth, 89, 95; as
    director, 90–91, 92; "exile"
    after Swift apology, 87, 88;
    extended family, 10, 50; and
    fashion, 5, 6, 14, 22, 27, 78–79,
    87, 96; first studio, 15–17, 23,
    64; and hip-hop, 21, 29, 81,
    99; in elementary school, 9; in

high school, 14, 81; injured in
car crash, 33–34, 35, 38, 69; in
middle school, 13; lyrics, 6, 19,
38, 41, 57, 59, 68–69, 76, 90–91,
93, 98; mentors, 17; mixing,
24; name, 7–8; problems with
alcohol, 77, 87; as producer,
29, 32, 33, 39, 42, 68; and
rap, 13–14, 23, 29, 32–33, 36,
39, 42–43, 68–69, 81, 82, 99;
relationship with his father, 6,
10; relationship with his mother,
8–9, 10–12, 19, 20, 23, 56,
73–74, 76, 82, 88; response to
Hurricane Katrina, 61–63; at
Roc-A-Fella Records, 25, 26–29;
and social commentary, 6, 10,
50, 53, 55, 57, 58, 68, 93–94,
98, 99
West, Ray, 7–8, 10, 69
Williams, Portwood "Buddy," Sr., 10
Wilson, Dion. *See* No I.D.
Wonder, Stevie, 9, 58

Youth Movement Records, 43

PHOTO ACKNOWLEDGMENTS

The images in this book are used with the permission of: © Robert Hanashiro/USA TODAY, pp. 1, 3, 45, 46, 75 (bottom left and bottom right), 82, 107; © Sayre Berman/CORBIS, p. 4; AP Photo/Julio Cortez, p. 5; AP Photo, pp. 7, 67; © Ray Tamarra/Getty Images, p. 8 (left); © Noel Vasquez/Getty Images, p. 8 (right); © David Fenton/Archive Photos/Getty Images, p. 11; © Jeff Kravitz/FilmMagic/Getty Images, pp. 13, 84; Seth Poppel Yearbook Library, p. 15; © Sam Diephuis/CORBIS, p. 16; © Stephen Lovekin/FilmMagic/Getty Images, p. 17; © iStockphoto.com/Steve Geer, p. 18; © Jemal Countess/Getty Images, p. 20; © Kevin Mazur/WireImage/Getty Images, pp. 22, 30, 38, 41, 50, 54, 58, 68, 76 (top), 81, 90, 93, 98; © Michael Ochs Archives/CORBIS, p. 23; AP Photo/Erik S. Lesser, p. 24 (top); © Rick Williams/USA TODAY, p. 24 (bottom); © Ryan McVay/Stone+/Getty Images, p. 25; © Jonathan Mannion/CORBIS, p. 26; © Larry Ford/CORBIS, p. 27; © Frank Micelotta/Getty Images, pp. 32, 43; © Johnny Nunez/WireImage/Getty Images, pp. 33, 72; AP Photo/Jim Cooper, p. 35; © Raymond Boyd/Michael Ochs Archives/Getty Images, p. 37 (top); © Theo Wargo/WireImage/Getty Images, p. 37 (bottom); © Tim Mosenfelder/Getty Images, p. 40; © Richard Corkery/NY Daily News Archive/Getty Images, p. 42; AP Photo/Mark J. Terrill, pp. 44, 70; AP Photo/David Drapkin, p. 48; © Jack Gruber/USA TODAY, p. 49 (top); © Jeff Gross/Getty Images, p. 49 (bottom); © Peter Kramer/Getty Images, p. 51; © J. Emilio Flores/ CORBIS, p. 52; AP Photo/Ben Curtis, p. 53; © Handout/USA TODAY, p. 55; © Dan MacMedan/ USA TODAY, p. 56; © Dana Edelson/NBC/Getty Images, p. 60; © Marko Georgiev/Getty Images, p. 61; AP Photo/Susan Walsh, p. 62; WENN/Newscom, p. 64; AP Photo/Jon Super, p. 66; AP Photo/Dan Steinberg, p. 71; © Arnaldo Magnani/Getty Images, p. 73; AP Photo/ Kevork Djansezian, p. 75 (top); © Dominique Charriau/WireImage/Getty Images, p. 76 (bottom); © Marty Melville/Getty Images, p. 77; © Eric Ryan/Getty Images, p. 78; London Entertainment/Splash/Newscom, p. 80; AP Photo/Jason DeCrow, p. 86; TakeOver Media, PacificCoastNews/Newscom, p. 87; © Jen Maler/Retna Ltd., p. 88; ZUMA Press/Newscom, p. 89; © Joe Corrigan/Getty Images, p. 91; © Walik Goshorn/Retna Ltd., p. 92; AP Photo/ Roc-A-Fella/Def Jam Recordings/Roc Nation, p. 94; © Timothy A. Clary/AFP/Getty Images, p. 95; © Pascal Le Segretain/Getty Images, p. 96; © Erika Goldring/Getty Images, p. 99; © H. Darr Beiser/USA TODAY, p. 101.

Front cover: Richard Young/Rex USA.

Back cover: © Kevin Mazur/WireImage/Getty Images.

Main body text set in USA TODAY Roman Regular 10.5/15.

ABOUT THE AUTHOR

Kayla Morgan is the author of several biographies and nonfiction books for young readers. She lives in New York City, where she teaches writing. She earned her master's degree in writing from the Vermont College of Fine Arts. She enjoys photography and hip-hop.